Discover What Really Happens on Those Exclusive Incentive Tours!

A funny story can happen anywhere, and *Humor Travels Well* proves it. Some of these stories are racy, some are educational. All are enjoyable and entertaining.

Humor is the one language that is truly universal. It is understood and appreciated in the Soviet Union and Scandinavia just as much as it is in Barbados or Beijing.

The author writes of incidents that occurred during his 27-year career as a travel professional. He takes the time during his story telling to relay tidbits of information about life in the Eastern Bloc countries before the Wall came tumbling down. He describes experiences in Asia and Australia and other exciting places because humor travels easily across continents.

Whether you're laughing or smiling, you'll be absorbed in the anecdotes from Rome and Rio, from Nassau and Nairobi.

The stories criss-cross the world. And you'll have fun traveling with them.

Believe it or not—these stories are even funnier the second or third time you read them!

About the Author

Peter B. Docherty is president of Northwestern Incentive Services, a sales incentive company headquartered in Edina, Minnesota.

He is a native of Glasgow, Scotland, and is a graduate of a Scottish college where he majored in journalism. He was a travel writer for a daily newspaper in Michigan for several years before entering the sales incentive business in Detroit in 1963.

Pete has traveled extensively around the world and has visited places many people would have trouble finding on a map. It would be easier to list the areas he *hasn't* visited than the ones he has been to.

He is now working on his first novel—and, of course, it's about the incentive business.

TO BOB RIPPE...

... who also knows
the joys -- and tribulations
-- of travel.

Pete Docherty

11-26-91

HUMOR
TRAVELS WELL

Tours de Farce

By Pete Docherty

Galde Press, Inc.
PO Box 65611, St. Paul, MN, U.S.A. 55165

First Edition
First Printing

Cover Design by Sheila Macho

Illustrations by Jack Adair

Canadian-born cartoonist Jack Adair started his professional career in the fourth grade by selling full-color drawings of the Disney and Warner Bros. cartoon characters to fellow classmates for a dime. Jack feels that making people laugh is rewarding to both the one who sees the humor and the one who creates it. He accomplishes this not only with his cartoons, but also as a writer/composer of novelty songs.

 Printed on recycled paper.

Galde Press, Inc.
PO Box 65611
St. Paul, MN 55165-0611

Contents

Introduction

The stories that appear in this book are true. They happened in the countries as portrayed. The names of the trip directors, clients and others have either been omitted or changed to protect their guilt. In some cases, I have deliberately not mentioned the locale in which an incident occurred. This was done to prevent embarrassment to local officials; however, the incident, I assure you, did happen.

When I started in sales incentives back in

1963, I quickly learned that almost every trip yielded humorous and interesting stories. I decided to jot down some of the funnier things that took place, with the ultimate objective of writing a book.

Today, there are many companies in the sales incentive industry. There are three giants; the others are in the small to medium size. Sales incentive companies are motivation firms that assist clients in increasing sales and profits through the implementation of marketing campaigns. Simply, quotas are set, and if participants meet that quota, they and their spouses or guests are treated to trips to Las Vegas, Paris, Hong Kong or wherever the client decides he would like to take his winners.

The client may also elect to offer merchandise as a reward rather than travel, and, in fact, merchandise has the bigger slice of the incentive dollar.

While the sales incentive business is relatively new, having really only taken hold immediately after World War II, the industry has grown dramatically and has been rising steadily each year. The money expended by U.S. companies in 1990 to increase or maintain their market share has been estimated at almost $10 billion.

Glossary

To help you understand some of the esoteric terms employed in the incentive business, and, consequently, used in this book, explanations are given below.

Convip

The contact VIP of the company sponsoring the incentive travel program. The Convip may not be the highest ranking company official on the trip, but is the one responsible for working with the trip director to approve any deviations from the program and all additional expenditures.

Trip Director

Employee of the incentive firm who accompanies groups to oversee the trips and insures that they operate smoothly and according to the contents of the contract. They are also known as TDs.

Travel Staff

Employees of the incentive company who accompany the group and work under the supervision of the trip director. Travel staff are also known as trip directors although the term is usually reserved for the one in charge.

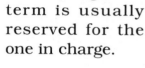

Sponsoring Company

The company that offers the trip or merchandise to its distributors, dealers or salesmen as rewards for meeting the set quotas.

Inspection Trip

The trip taken by an official of the sponsoring company, and accompanied by a representative of the incentive firm, to go over the itinerary on site. During an inspection trip, the client examines all parts of the program (e.g., the hotel, restaurants, nightclubs, etc.) that will be offered his group. If the official finds something not to his liking, he will change it accordingly.

Land Agents

Employees of local travel agencies in the c o u n t r i e s where the trips take place, and used by incentive houses to  confirm all parts of the program. The land agents work with the trip director throughout the program and are responsible, among other things, for arranging the buses, guides, tours and restaurants.

Recently, these travel agencies have acquired the more pretentious name of Destination Management Company or DMC for short.

Fam Trip

A trip to a domestic or foreign destination to acquaint travel people with the area and to help them evaluate whether the locale has sufficient appeal for group tours. Fam trips are usually sponsored by tourist offices in conjunction with airlines, hotels and land agents.

Campaign

The period in which all eligible participants purchase items or make sales to meet the quota set by the sponsoring company. The campaigns can range from 30 days to two years but the most common length is one year.

Account Executive

A synonym for a sales-person. The account executive is the one who sells the incentive program to clients and who serves as the intermediary between the incentive company and the client for all parts of the program. Account executives are also responsible for developing or assisting in the formulation of marketing plans (or rules structures) for the campaign.

Trip Director *after* the tour.

The Lost Bag

If there is one problem trip directors detest, it is lost bags. It is the bane of the travel business. Even the friendliest and quietest guest soon becomes irate when his or his wife's bags are lost. And invariably it's the bag with his sports gear (if the group is staying at a resort) or his best suit (if it's a big city).

The stories that I have listened to go from the ridiculous to the sublime and back again.

With some, the lost bag contained all the

wife's jewelry, 24-carat gold chains, diamond rings, pearl necklaces and irreplaceable bracelets. Or the bag had her brand new Bill Blass dress which was purchased just for the trip and hadn't even been worn yet.

And there's the husband who wore his everyday watch on the flight but packed his gold Rolex to wear at special functions during the trip. And, of course, he had two brand new tailor-made, silk suits in the errant case.

I have often wished that just once I could witness the lost bag, when found, being opened to see if it really did contain all of the items the guests claimed.

*   *   *

We had a group in Barbados, and all the luggage had been delivered to the rooms when an attractive woman approached the hospitality desk.

"Have all the bags been sent up to the rooms?" she inquired. I told her that they had.

"Oh, dear," she sighed, "then I'm afraid I've lost one."

I tried to pacify her by assuring her that lost bags are found 99 per cent of the time. She revealed that the lost bag was a small, pale-blue cosmetics case, that her name was

Debbie Jones and that she was in room 243.

"Give us an hour and I'm sure we'll have found it by then," I consoled her.

Five minutes later, Ron Carter, the Convip, came over to the hospitality desk and said, "I understand that Ms. Jones has lost her bag." I confirmed that she had, but that I was sure we would soon find it.

"Good," he mumbled and moved on.

After another 30 minutes had elapsed, Ms. Jones returned to ask if her bag had been found yet, and I had to inform her that we were still searching for it, but that I was confident of its being located.

It began to form a pattern. Within five minutes, Carter stopped at the desk, not to inquire if the bag was still lost, but to tell me he knew that it was still missing.

"You've got to find it," he said, almost pleadingly. He wanted to know what efforts were being made to recover it. Every incentive house uses the same systems. Someone is sent to the airport to check whether the group's special bag tag has been inadvertently torn off the case and so has not been collected by the porters. Another walks up and down the hotel's hallways to check whether the bag has been sent to the wrong room and left outside the door. There are more, but suffice it to say we had implemented most of them with no luck.

It was nearing the hour for the scheduled cocktail party when Ms. Jones sauntered over to the hospitality desk.

"Still no sign of it?"

"Not yet," I replied. "Is there anything in the case that you need for this evening's function, such as makeup?" I asked. "If there is something you need, buy it in the hotel, give me the receipt and I'll reimburse you."

"Oh, no, nothing like that," she whispered, obviously very dejected, and walked slowly away.

I waited for Carter to turn up, and sure enough, he soon came storming over. He motioned for me to follow him, and we proceeded to a spot which afforded complete privacy.

"Look," he began, "do you want a happy VIP or one that's really angry?"

I assured him that I wanted a happy VIP.

"OK, then," he continued, "here's what you do. You send every available member of your staff to look for Ms. Jones' case. Ms. Jones and I know each other very well. Do you know what I mean? Her birth control pills are in that case, and if it's not found, I get no lovin'. If I don't get any lovin', I'll be unbearable. Got the picture?"

"Perfectly, Mr. Carter. We'll find it."

What gall that guy has, I thought. I knew he had his wife with him, and here he was playing patty-cake with another woman. And his bosses and their spouses were on the same trip!

Another system used to find a lost bag is to ask everyone in the group, when assembled together for a function, to let the travel staff know if they had a bag delivered to their room that didn't belong to them.

And that is how we found Ms. Jones' cosmetics case. And that is how we had a happy VIP—and a happy ending.

Dancing was scheduled to follow the dinner that evening, and I was standing talking to some of the guests just inside the entrance to the ballroom when Carter and Ms. Jones danced by.

He caught my eye and suddenly the thumb of his right hand, firmly holding Ms. Jones' back, jerked up and he smiled.

I overheard two of the wives discussing Carter. "He's such a wonderful man, isn't he?" one said to the other. "He makes sure that the single women have a chance to enjoy dancing, too. He's so thoughtful and considerate."

"Yes," the other agreed, "I wish there were more like him."

The Too-Compact
Compact

Beverly Anderson was smart and talented. She was also, unquestionably, one of the brightest travel people I've known over the years. Unfortunately, Beverly had a weight problem that I am sure prevented her from rising through the ranks to more important positions.

This is a euphemistic way of saying Beverly was very obese. In fact, she was so huge, she had to travel first class on airplanes and even then had difficulty fitting her enormous frame into the wider seat in the front section of the aircraft. I'm sure it is apocryphal, but I was told that in her later years, she had to reserve two first class seats to accommodate her.

It had been about two years since I had last seen Beverly when I ran into her in Rome. I had a luncheon appointment with Luigi Mangiani, the director of sales of a large hotel in the Eternal City.

When I approached the reception desk, I asked the clerk if he would notify Mr. Mangiani that I was downstairs. A few seconds later, I was asked to go up to the sales office on the second floor.

The assistant director of sales, Vincenzo, a pleasant fellow whom I also knew, greeted me at the top of the stairs and said an old friend of mine was with his boss and that I was to go right in.

"Peter," cried Beverly, "how nice to see you again after all this time."

An appraising glance revealed that, if anything, Beverly had grown even heavier since our last meeting. After a few pleasantries had been exchanged, the director of sales invited Beverly to join us for lunch, but she declined saying she already had a luncheon appointment.

"Then I must insist on having you chauffeured to your appointment in one of the hotel cars," he gallantly offered.

He asked Vincenzo to "line up a Mercedes to take Beverly downtown."

Vincenzo left the office to arrange the transportation, and we resumed our conversation, catching up on what each of us had been doing since we had last seen each other.

After several minutes, the director of sales suggested that we walk Beverly to the front door where the car would be waiting.

We had just left his office when Vincenzo, wearing a worried look on his face, returned and spoke to Luigi in Italian and in an agitated manner.

I could hear Luigi's voice rise in anger before he returned to Beverly with a contrived smile on his face. "Beverly, I am so sorry, but our three Mercedes are being used. May I get you a cab?"

Before Beverly could answer, Vincenzo broke in with an explanation that he could get one of the hotel's two VW beetles. "They are not so grand, but they're available," Vincenzo said innocently.

"Well, that's not a problem," said Beverly. "I can ride in the VW. After all, I'm not so important that I have to have a Mercedes."

Luigi's face fell. He glowered at Vincenzo as if to say, "You idiot. Why did you have to say that?"

Turning to Beverly, he pointed out that a VW was not comfortable enough for her and that it was not the kind of car in which the hotel put its valued clients.

By this time, Beverly knew that it was not the car that was the problem, but that nobody thought she could fit into a VW. (I didn't think she could fit into a *stretched* Mercedes!) Despite Luigi's protestations, Beverly had made up her mind to ride in the VW.

The hotel had a very popular doorman with a round, florid face, a luxurious mustache and an omnipresent smile. When he saw us approach, he walked towards us, tipped his cap and asked if he might call a cab.

"No, Umberto," the director of sales said sadly. "We have a car coming for the Signora."

At that moment, the VW pulled up at the front door and Umberto ran around to the driver to ask him to move it forward because "the Mercedes is coming."

"No, Umberto," said Luigi, "that is the car for the Signora."

Umberto looked at Beverly and at the VW, and said with a grin (undiplomatically, some might say), "I know you are jesting with me." Then, as he saw the piercing look on Beverly's face, he recovered beautifully by saying, "This hotel never puts its important guests in a VW."

A visibly upset Luigi assured the doorman that he was not joking. He was greatly embarrassed and fully aware that the next few minutes were going to be extremely trying.

Umberto held the door open and Beverly strode forward. She put a foot inside the car, then tried to turn around and sit in the front seat—but it didn't work. She withdrew after much struggling and attempted to point her spacious derriere toward the seat and *back* in. This, too, proved unsuccessful.

Then the driver suggested that she enter the car by stretching her hands forward while he grabbed them and pulled her in. She concurred; as the driver pulled, beads of sweat appeared on his forehead.

Umberto rushed forward and placed his white-gloved hands squarely on Beverly's buttocks and pushed.

Beverly was greatly embarrassed. "Do you mind?" she shouted at Umberto, giving him a withering glance. The doorman reddened as he withdrew his hands and apologized for his temporary lapse of good manners.

By now, Beverly was firmly ensconced in the VW, but not in the conventional way. Her head was almost in the lap of the driver, when he took his seat, and her ample rear end protruded beyond where the window would have been if it had not been lowered to provide more room.

One can only imagine what pedestrians must have thought as the VW sped through the streets of Rome with a large posterior filling the window frame. No doubt they thought it was a mischievous kid "mooning" them.

I tried to find out how Beverly was extricated from the VW when she reached her destination, but I was never able to do so. I do know that Vincenzo, who joined us for lunch, did not enjoy his meal. Luigi cursed him in Italian, adding in English several times—for my benefit, no doubt—"stupid son-of-a-bitch!"

The Piano

Music may indeed soothe the savage breast, but sometimes it can cause more trouble than comfort.

We had a group in Marbella on the sunny coast of Spain, and the sponsoring company's president was reputed to be an accomplished musician. A company vice president told me that the president was a talented pianist, but two dealers said he was only a couple of lessons beyond "Chopsticks."

I was made aware that the president

always invited some of his key dealers to his suite after the last evening's function for drinks and a few tunes on the piano.

The Convip motioned to me in the lobby on the next to last morning and ordered me to make some inquiries concerning the use of a piano for the president's penthouse suite.

I spoke to the hotel's director of sales, who informed me that the two pianos in the hotel would be in use at the time the instrument was needed. He suggested I contact a music company in Malaga, some 30 miles away, and arrange to rent one.

It wasn't too much trouble to organize the piano, and it was trucked out to the hotel early in the morning of the evening it would be required.

And then the fun began. First, the president's suite was on the top floor of the hotel — on the eighth floor to be precise.

The workmen who trucked over the piano were surprised (no, shocked is a better word) when they learned that it had to be transported up eight floors. They wheeled it over to the freight elevator, but after much struggling they found it was never going to be moved that way.

Becoming more scientific, one of the workmen located a measuring tape which revealed that the passenger elevators were even smaller than those used for freight.

Unless it was carried up the eight flights of stairs, the dealers would face a music-less evening (which, undoubtedly, would have made it more enjoyable for them.)

The weight of the piano was considered, the turns in the stairways were measured, and again it proved to be an impossible task.

*   *   *

But hope (and the pleadings of a worried Convip) refused to let the project die. One of the movers made a joke about hiring a crane and having the piano hoisted up to the penthouse. Everyone laughed—except the Convip.

"Could it be done?" he asked. The laughter stopped and several puzzled looks were exchanged before I asked if he was serious. He assured us he was deadly serious, but asked that I get a price for him.

The hotel's director of sales was brought into the act, and he came up with the name of a construction company in nearby Torremolinos. To help me in my predicament, he made a couple of calls before speaking with the manager of a building company.

"Is this a joke?" the senor asked, not sure whether he was having his leg pulled. "Give me your number at the hotel and I'll call you back. I want to be sure that this is a legitimate call."

He took the hotel official's name and number and returned the call almost immediately.

Satisfied, the senor muttered that he had never heard such a request in his 40-odd years in the business. But he was finally convinced and gave us a steep price .

"Do it," the Convip said, unhesitatingly, and the piano was as good as in the suite—I thought!

Permission was requested of the police to have the huge crane moved through town. Police cars were assigned to lead and follow the crane as it moved slowly to its destiny. Eventually, the equipment was readied just to the side of the hotel's lawn and the piano was introduced to its "helper." The hotel's general manager, who had now entered the picture, was visibly perturbed and insisted that no damage be done to his gardens.

The crane's hooks were attached, and the piano slowly rose as more than 100 people —guests and locals—gathered to watch its progress.

One floor, two floors, three, four. It rose to the sixth before it slipped from one of the crane's hooks, but it did not fall. Gasps escaped from the crowd below, and they scattered to safety in anticipation of the piano's imminent fall, smashing into a thousand pieces with debris flying dangerously in all directions.

But the piano held, although its continuance upward was deemed unsafe. It was slowly returned to the lawn.

The crane's hooks were rearranged and strong chains were also affixed to be sure that, this time, the piano would not evade the clutches of the predatorial machine.

By this time, the crowd had enlarged to around 200 and a newspaper photographer was furiously clicking away while undoubtedly hoping for a disaster and much better photographs.

The crane operator pushed forward a lever and the piano once more attempted its climb to the eighth floor.

The crowd cheered and applauded while ice cream and soft drink vendors moved their carts onto the lawn. The manager, now becoming apoplectic, was trying to find hotel security to eject the hawkers. It proved to be a hopeless task, and the number of vendors was augmented by balloon men and others who had moved up from the beach where they had been trying to sell straw hats and wooden carvings.

By now the hotel's bars had emptied; the topers had joined the mob on the lawn to add their support to the cheering crowd.

Two police cars drew up to the street, unable to approach the front door of the property due to the enormous crowd that had now amassed. As they collared the vendors and tried to lead them away, a fight broke out and an assortment of items from carvings to hot dogs spilled onto the lawn and was trampled underfoot as multicolored balloons became untethered and floated heavenward, quickly passing the slowly ascending piano.

A paddy wagon was called and, as the police tried to force the recalcitrants into the vehicle, other locals came to their rescue.

A fire department vehicle, sirens blaring, soon arrived. Out rolled the hoses and the firemen began spraying the belligerents, who quickly dispersed.

The piano was now precariously perched alongside the balcony of the penthouse. Alas, more trouble was in store. The windows of the suite were just short of the space needed to move in the piano. The hotel's engineer, however, carefully calculated that, if the glass doors were taken out, it would be possible to squeeze the instrument through.

The doors were soon removed, the piano was eased into the suite and the doors were replaced.

Success!

While this incredible series of events had been occurring, the entire group was on a full-day tour to Granada. They returned to the hotel in the late afternoon, completely unaware of the seemingly incessant problems caused by the president's desire to entertain some of his guests.

A few members of the group noted that there must have been a party on the lawn. Several commented that it had to have been a wild one because the lawn and flower beds were almost totally chewed up.

The group's final night program was to include a cocktail party and an awards banquet followed by the presentation. It was obvious from the condition of many as they disembarked from the coaches after their tour that they might not be able to negotiate the stairs to the stage to accept their awards.

Worse, it was doubtful if the president would be able to stand up long enough to present the plaques!

I learned later that not only had wine been liberally poured at the lunch in Granada but that, on the return, the lead bus had stopped at a private home in a village to enable one of the group to use the bathroom.

A family had been kind enough to allow the tourist to use their facilities. As he left the toilet, he smelled the unmistakable heady aroma of wine and asked his hosts if they made their own brand. An affirmative answer opened up the conversation and culminated in his purchasing 12 bottles—four for each of the three buses.

It is not uncommon in southern European countries for families to make their own wine, but it is recommended that such wine be allowed to age a little before being drunk.

In its early stage, after being bottled, the liquid is referred to as "green wine." Moreover, an unfortunate consequence of consuming wine that has not been allowed to mature is that it upsets the stomach and induces a condition that is generally known as "Montezuma's Revenge."

Needless to say, all of the wine was consumed by the time the buses reached the hotel.

On returning to their rooms, the key dealers of the group found elegantly printed cards that had been distributed earlier in the day. The cards informed them that the president and his wife wished to have them attend a piano recital in the penthouse suite that evening after the official function.

*　　*　　*

The cocktail party passed without incident,

although I thought the atmosphere was considerably subdued from the reception they enjoyed on their first evening on the sunny coast of Spain. What's more, I don't ever remember seeing so many people leave a cocktail party or rise from a dinner table and head for the rest rooms and do it as frequently as that group did that night.

After the banquet, the vice president strode to the podium and briefly mentioned that the president was not feeling too well, unfortunately, and that he would substitute for him in making the awards.

The president's wife spoke with the couples who had been invited to the penthouse suite that evening and apologized that their planned soiree had to be cancelled. It amused me that those with whom she spoke showed real concern on their faces and expressed the hope that the president would be well enough to travel back to the States the following morning.

Every one of them knew that their beloved leader was three sheets to the wind, and I am convinced that they were secretly delighted that they would not have to be subjected to an ear-rending evening of amateurish piano playing.

And so the piano was not touched. The president never knew the monumental problems that had occurred in trying to place a piano in his suite.

As the manager vehemently refused to allow the same method to be used to remove the piano, the Convip magnanimously purchased the instrument and gave it to the hotel as a gift for all the trouble that had been caused.

A generous check was also given to the hotel to compensate for the disaster that had ruined its gardens and lawn.

"I trust the evening went off well and that everyone enjoyed Mr. Caroll's playing?" the manager said unctuously, now that he had an extra piano in his hotel.

I was standing close by and the Convip was obviously too embarrassed to tell the manager what had really happened.

"It was a most enjoyable evening and well worth all the trouble it took to have the piano delivered to his suite," he said with as straight a face as he could muster.

To this day, there is a Kimball piano in the penthouse suite of a hotel in Marbella.

English Theatre

There is a true saying in the incentive travel business that you can't have a bad trip in London, Switzerland or Hawaii. All three are superb destinations that have a plethora of attractions to keep tourists happy and contented.

But untoward situations do occasionally occur that make even such Utopian destinations problematic. A good example happened in London in the early '70s.

It is the consensus that London is one of

the greatest cities in the world. It has an abundance of sophistication to appeal to the highbrow and a sufficiency of earthly pleasures to please those who need to get away from their hometowns to have some real fun. And for all those in between, London has cricket, lawn bowling and tiddlywinks!

The winners and spouses of an insurance company's incentive campaign were in London for a six-night stay. The itinerary was so full of activities that a last-minute request by the company president to include a theater visit proved difficult to accommodate. But a presidential request is not something that is blithely dismissed, as many a cowering Convip will attest.

The group's well-balanced program included carefully planned functions every night, and the only way to comply with the request (that is, the order) was to eliminate a function and substitute the theater. London theaters raise their curtains at 8:00 P.M., making it very difficult for a group to have an enjoyable and unhurried meal and then transfer by bus to arrive before the show begins.

Londoners usually have something light before the theater and a more substantial meal afterwards. This would have been easy for us to arrange, but we had already paid for the sumptuous meals in elegant surroundings at various venues in the London area.

Nevertheless, the Convip and I conferred with our London land agent and asked him to ascertain if it was possible to purchase 150 choice seats at any top theater. But nothing was available, not a surprising revelation when one considers how very popular London theater is.

But all was not doomed. The Convip's job could be saved. Our agent came up with an answer. The itinerary called for dinner at one of the palatial mansions that dot the outskirts of London.

*   *   *

The banquet was to be the epitome of elegance, with white-gloved servants, candles and flowers on the tables and a chamber quartet playing background music that everyone agreed "fit the occasion"—a euphemism for "thank God this is the only night we have to listen to this." Normally, such a regal affair would leisurely stretch out to 10:30 P.M. or later.

Our agent pointed out that this particular mansion was only three miles from a theater where 150 tickets could be purchased. While the theater was not considered one of the top "legitimate houses," it was where Sir Alec

Guinness, Sir Ralph Richardson and Sir Laurence Olivier and many other luminaries of the British stage had performed earlier in their careers. Further, the previously arranged time of 7:00 P.M. for the banquet could be brought forward to 5:30 P.M.

The idea was sold to the president, who, although disappointed that his group would not be seeing "Fiddler on the Roof" or something similar, was pleased that at least "his people" would experience the professionalism of British theater.

After the dinner at the mansion on that soon-to-become highly memorable evening, the group boarded the buses for the brief ride to the theater. Everyone was seated; the curtain rose; the play began.

The plot of the play involved the daughter of a king who was betrothed to a wealthy prince. The princess, alas, did not love the prince and had been forced into the match by her scheming father.

But princesses can be as Machiavellian as kings, and she took unto herself a lover. Worse, he was a commoner. (Even worse, everyone in the audience was convinced the lover would have been happier chasing the prince!)

The prince, learning that his bride-to-be was having trysts in the woods, was deter-

mined to put an end to them. He followed the princess to her rendezvous and listened as she soliloquized about the physical attributes of her lover as she awaited his arrival. Unable to contain his rage, the prince leaped from behind some cardboard bushes and plunged his dagger into her chest. Hearing the footsteps of the approaching lover, he hastily departed.

The princess lay still on the proscenium. The commoner, reaching the scene, reacted with horror as he saw his beloved motionless on the floor. He rushed over, knelt beside her and cradled her head in his arms. Slowly, he lifted his tear-stained face to the heavens and cried: "She's dead; she's dead. What will I do?"

From the "cheap seats" in the third balcony came a suggestion:

"Fuck 'er while she's warm."

American Slang

There is no country in the world that is more prolific in the production of slick sayings than the United States. In the last few years, there have appeared such phrases as "No Sweat," "Stay Cool," "Get Real," and words like "Wimp" and "Doof."

These words and phrases have even gone far beyond the U.S. and are now part of young people's lexicons in all English-speaking nations. In England, in particular, you hear American slang frequently spicing the language of the locals.

But when these phrases reach non-English-speaking countries, the people there who speak English as another language can often be confused by the strange combinations.

Let me give you one example.

I was sent to Buenos Aires, Argentina, for the purpose of evaluating the city as a possible site for a program for a group of tractor dealers. One of the writers from our Creative Department, Don Dixon, accompanied me. He was assigned the task of writing promotional copy to be distributed to all the participants throughout the campaign, and he wanted to see firsthand what he would be promoting.

We were met at the airport by our land agent, a young woman named Nila, who told me she spoke five languages. She mentioned that she had found English not only the easiest to learn but also the one she most enjoyed speaking.

"It is a rich language with so many synonyms that I find it easier to describe situations in English than in any other language," she informed me.

Nila spent the first two days showing us hotels and restaurants as well as some of the landmarks of her beautiful city. Buenos Aires is a metropolis of exceptional grandeur, with long, sprawling boulevards bedecked with colorful flowers and plants. Typical of its Spanish heritage, there are many plazas, fountains, stucco houses juxtaposed with modern skyscrapers and elegant shopping malls throughout the city.

In many ways, Buenos Aires reminds the visitor of Madrid, not only in its architecture, but in the customs and lifestyles of its people.

We returned to the hotel late one night after having looked at several nightclubs and discos. We had heard the music for every tango dance and seen every tango step that ever existed.

Nila had noticed our exhaustion brought on by long hours in the air traveling to Argentina as well as by our busy itinerary.

"I'll give you a break tomorrow," she said. "We're going out to a ranch to see gauchos at work and to let you have a look at some of our magnificent pampas. Let's leave at 10 o'clock, OK?"

It sounded great to Don and me. "Ten o'clock will be just fine," we responded.

We had a late breakfast next morning and finished about 10 minutes to 10:00. "Listen, I have to take a dump," Don said. "Explain to Nila that I'll be just a few minutes late."

I strolled down to the lobby, and soon Nila showed up with a car and driver.

"Good morning," she said in her natural, breezy way. "Did you sleep well?"

I assured her that I had had a very restful evening and was ready for the gauchos and the pampas.

"Where's Don?" she asked.

"Oh, he'll be down shortly," I told her. "He's having a dump."

She smiled and asked: "What do you mean 'dump'? I have never heard the word used that way before."

Although I used the word accidentally, I was surprised when she caught on to the American slang. I hadn't anticipated her keen interest in our colloquialisms nor an explanation of what the word meant.

"Oh," I stammered, trying to come up with the right words, "that means a good rest. You know, dump yourself in bed. Don was still a little tired after breakfast and decided to take another nap."

She immediately wrote it down in a book she took her from purse. "I really do enjoy American idioms," she cooed.

Don was spotted coming through the front door, looking relaxed and ready for the day ahead of us.

"Good morning, Don, did you have a good dump?" Nila asked him in all innocence, with a smile on her face, positive that Don would

be impressed with her knowledge of our idioms.

I thought Don was going to have a seizure. His face reddened and he looked really embarrassed; he didn't know what to say.

"Well, tell Nila that you have had a most enjoyable dump, Don," I encouraged him.

He couldn't believe his ears; he was completely dumbfounded and looked at me with a not-so-strange look of anger on his face.

"I explained to Nila that dump means a 'sleep,' and she says she loves to collect American slang."

Don's embarrassment eased slightly, and I could see that he caught on right away.

"Oh, yes indeed," he responded, "I had a truly great dump."

When we arrived at the ranch, Don and I excused ourselves to go to the washroom. This was the first time we had been alone since we left the hotel, and Don immediately quizzed me on what happened. When I explained, he began to laugh.

"You took a helluva chance that she didn't understand our slang," he commented. I told him that the word really just slipped out, and I reminded him that it was he who used it in the first place. I wouldn't have used it if he hadn't put the word in my mind.

Suddenly, Don broke into a fit of laughter,

so much so that the tears ran down his cheeks.

"You're thinking of something." I said. "What is it?"

I just thought of a scenario," he went on. "Can you see Nila on a bus full of American tourists returning from a long day tour and she says to the tired group: 'Well, we're almost at the hotel now, and you'll have time for a nice dump before we go out to dinner.' "

I pictured the scene, and I too couldn't stop laughing.

India

Incentive travel people are frequently invited by foreign airlines and tourist offices to visit their countries in the hope that their lands will be found appealing enough to recommend to clients.

It's nigh impossible to accept all of the invitations, but those with particular appeal and those to unusual and unique destinations are always taken.

One afternoon, I got a call from the president's secretary, who told me the boss wanted to see me in his office.

"Something really important has come up and I can't go to India," he said. "I want you to take my place. I've cleared it with the tourist office and Air India." He went on to advise me to get shots for typhoid, cholera, yellow fever and tetanus immediately. The departure date was only 10 days off.

I had known that the president was going to India, and that he had been receiving his shots at decent intervals. I was forced to have mine all at once, with boosters a few days later. My arms puffed up so badly, I had to apply ice packs to control the swellings.

The trip was a very special one in that the invitation had, ostensibly, come from Indira Gandhi, the Prime Minister, and during the visit, I was scheduled to have afternoon tea with her. (Unfortunately, this never materialized. She had to fly unexpectedly to Ceylon, now Sri Lanka, on the day of the appointment, but I did have tea with the Ministers of Tourism and Transportation, both members of the Indian Cabinet.)

The purpose of the visit was to assess India's potential for incentive groups. The president of our company was one of the founders of the incentive travel industry and was recognized as a top authority. I was chosen to represent him more for my ability to write reports than for my expertise. I was certainly not in the same league as he in terms of experience or knowledge of the business.

Throughout the trip, I was accompanied by Alan Yarrow, an official of Air India based in Detroit. Alan's joyous sense of humor and vibrant personality made the odyssey even more enjoyable.

The trip provided so much material for stories that I have written them as separate incidents.

1. The English Ladies

We were to spend a night in Agra, where man's supreme monument to love (or as an Indian put it, "Man's greatest erection for a woman"), the Taj Mahal, is located. We took the Taj Express from New Delhi and ensconced ourselves in spacious, comfortable, first-class seats. The train was certainly one of the most elegant on which I have ever traveled.

Our huge compartment had eight seats, with our own obsequious waiter to respond to our every need. The only other occupants were two very refined, sophisticated English ladies who were definitely of the upper crust.

They had rare, colloquial virtues, and the conversation was stimulating and enlightening. They told us they had lived in India for many years, and gave Alan and me a greater feel for the country by imparting "do's and "don'ts" and helpful hints, and by suggesting places that must be visited.

*   *   *

The train moved slowly, not exceeding 35 miles an hour. This in itself is strange, because the Indian automobile drivers race at dangerous speeds on badly-constructed roads.

My seat in the compartment faced the direction of travel, allowing me to see where we were going.

Suddenly, I almost choked. There ahead, on a bluff that would put him at eye level and about five feet from the window, was a man with his white robe raised, exposing his dark brown buttocks.

He was squatting, relieving himself beside the track. To prevent an embarrassing situation and with only a few seconds to distract the ladies' attention, I blurted out, "Oh, look over there," and pointed to the scenery on the

other side of the carriage.

As luck would have it, at that very moment a bull was engaged in an activity with a cow to which one does not draw attention.

"Oh, yes," one of the ladies muttered perfunctorily, not wanting to completely ignore the incident, yet making it clear that this was not the sort of topic that strangers discussed.

*   *   *

I was mortified. It would have been better to have taken a chance on letting them see the Indian defecating, actually a fairly common sight. At least, I would not have made such a fool of myself.

The ladies cooled considerably after my contretemps, and little conversation was held for the rest of the trip.

When we arrived at the station in Agra and were festooned with necklaces of geraniums, in the traditional welcome by the local tourist officials, Alan said out of the side of his mouth at the first opportunity he had to discuss the incident, "Why in hell did you point out the bull screwing the cow? I didn't know what to say I was so embarrassed!"

When I explained, we both laughed so hard our hosts must have thought we were idiots.

2. The Snake Charmer

I have always been terrified of snakes. Their very proximity gives me the chills and a palpitating heart.

I doubt if there is any country in the world with more snakes than India. In every city, village, community and at every monument where tourists gather, you see bow-legged little men, clad in their white robes and holding a sack in one hand and a flute in the other.

As soon as tourists are spotted, they rush over to "entertain" them. They drop the sack, blow into their flute and produce music that would make their cobras bite them rather than sway for them were it not for the fact that snakes are deaf.

As soon as the music starts, the cloth shakes and the cobra wriggles free and slowly rises as it oscillates to the movements of the flute. For some inexplicable reason, the fakirs think tourists equate this with a Dolly Parton performance.

I was staying at the Taj Mahal Hotel in Bombay, and I could not enter or leave the property without this one snake charmer rushing over to me. It got to be a game whether I could sneak in or out of the hotel without him seeing me.

Situated behind the Taj Mahal Hotel is the Gateway of India, an impressive archway built at the water's edge. It was here that King George V and Queen Mary, the first British monarchs ever to visit the colony, had stepped ashore on Indian soil in 1911. The monument was built by the Indian government to commemorate the occasion.

Alan and I were to visit the famous and somewhat notorious caves and temples on the island of Elephanta, just a few miles offshore. The caves are renowned for their sculptured figures of gods and goddesses entwined in scores of positions that prove to doubters that there are indeed countless ways to perform the love act.

As we mingled with about 30 other people waiting to board the ferry, we happened upon English nobility, Lord and Lady Ponsonby, who were combining business with pleasure on their visit to India.

In a word, Lord and Lady Ponsonby gave the impression that this was their party and all others were fortunate to be invited to join them. In fact, they had such a superior air that I wondered if they even knew that the stone effigies were engaged in love positions.

I mentioned this to Alan. He scoffed and said that Lady Ponsonby would say that it was art and Lord Ponsonby would ask, "Art who?"

The noble pair was talking to Alan and me about one of their businesses and, quite frankly, neither of us could recall afterward what they said. It's sometimes regarded as a joke that titled Britons talk as if their mouths were full of marbles. These two had agates.

As they spoke to us in their unintelligible fashion, I heard the unmistakable notes of the fakir's flute coming from right behind me. I could see the alarmed expressions on the faces of the Brits. They had turned white. I knew the reason for their pallid complexions: the fakir, his flute and cobra were right behind me.

Try though I did, I couldn't move. I wanted to run, but my legs would not respond to the shaky commands of my benumbed brain.

I stood there alone; the others had moved some distance away. Then I forced my head to turn, and there it was: the cobra's head was about three feet from me. Its beady eyes were focused on the flute, but were still cognizant of my proximity.

The temperature was about 110 degrees, but I actually shivered. Then the fakir lowered his flute towards the sack and the cobra followed its descent. The music stopped, and the serpent was stuffed inside the bag.

The fakir picked up the sack and smiled broadly at me, showing teeth that would have driven a dentist to despair.

*   *   *

The blood slowly returned to my limbs and my ability to issue verbal commands returned. And command I did. I have always believed that the constant use of profanity betrays a poor grasp of the English language and therefore have never been one of its prolific disciples. But on that sultry afternoon with Lord and Lady Ponsonby and other tourists looking on from several feet away, I cursed the fakir with the saltiest language I can ever recall

using. I even suggested a novel spot for his flute and his snake.

He took off, grasping his bag as I pursued him, still muttering expletives that I am sure he had never heard before but could understand, with a fair amount of accuracy, their meaning and intent.

Alan ran after me to restrain me from physically assaulting the fakir. When he succeeded in calming me, we returned to the Queen's Gate. Some people were smirking; others were genuinely shocked—I hoped by the incident and not by my language.

As for Lord and Lady Ponsonby, I'm certain they did not relay the incident to the Queen. They did not speak to me or acknowledge my presence for the rest of the tour.

And as for me, the incident ruined the beauty and excitement of the statues. No matter how provocative their position, no matter how stimulating their pose, I kept looking over my shoulder to make sure the fakir was not getting ready to tune up his flute.

3. The Maharajah

The itinerary called for me to stay one night at the Lake Palace Hotel in Udaipur. The hotel is one of the most unique properties I have ever seen, and no less an authority on the sybaritic things of this earth than James Bond agrees. A 007 movie was made at the hotel, and the endless luxury of the property was beautifully portrayed in the film *Octopussy*.

The hotel resembles a four-sided building that has been dropped in the center of a lake.

It has no real grounds or gardens and is accessible only by boat. The lake is manmade and the whole area is owned lock, stock and barrel by the Maharajah of Udaipur.

I was escorted to the top suite whose walls and ceilings were completely covered with mirrors. It is possible to see oneself from every angle, which made me wonder what its purpose was when first designed. In a word, ideal for James Bond's pursuits.

*　　*　　*

Several minutes after my arrival, there was a knock on the door which I opened to reveal a dusty-faced boy of about 16.

He was dressed in a satin coat and tight-fitting trousers and atop his head was a turban with a jewel in the center.

He held a velvet cushion with a silver tray on which rested an envelope. Inside was an embossed card inviting me to afternoon tea with His Excellency the Maharajah of Udaipur at precisely 4:00 P.M. in his palace. A boat and car would transport me. The card requested an answer. I accepted. Could anyone say "No" to all that?

Then the questions arose. What does one wear to such a function? How do I address him? What social niceties must I observe?

How would 007 handle all these?

Armed with the answers which I obtained from the hotel manager, Alan and I set off in trepidation to present ourselves to the great man. I wore a navy blue suit, long-sleeved shirt and tie in the 120-degree heat, and within minutes my neck chafed against my sodden collar. Alan was similarly attired, and similarly uncomfortable.

The launch took us to the shore where a Rolls Royce waited. We sank into the leather upholstered interior — for all of 90 seconds! We alighted before an enormous mahogany door. I struck it twice with the huge, iron knocker and a butler opened it to ask, in the politest of manners, our business.

My own discomfort was forgotten as I pitied the poor fellow in his immaculate attire of tails, stiff shirt and bow tie. He was the quintessential English butler.

When we presented our invitations, he led us along a high-ceilinged hallway, with huge animal heads looking down on us as though in inspection, to a shaded, outdoor patio at the rear of the palace.

After a few minutes, His Excellency the Maharajah appeared — dressed in a short-sleeved sports shirt, creaseless baggy slacks and what are known as jesus sandals!

We engaged in some small talk before being

regaled with tea and small pastries. Our social event lasted 20 minutes, and I thought it strange that the Maharajah did not suggest to Alan and me that we loosen our ties, doff our jackets and kick off our shoes. So I sweated in the heat and politely answered his questions on my reactions to India.

*   *   *

Then it was over. He rose; we rose. We shook hands, and the butler showed us out. And we returned to the hotel as we had come —by Rolls Royce and launch.

*   *   *

Strange, I thought, I love tea, but...

4. The Toilet

It is impossible, when describing India, not to mention its fabled Kashmir district. It is a land of incredible beauty, mirror-like lakes and towering mountains.

I was to stay two nights in its capital, Srinagar, and visit the resorts of Gulmarg and Tangmarg by climbing nearby mountains on a donkey. The journeys were brief, thank the Lord, as the asses (mine and the beast I was riding) couldn't have taken too much more.

My next appointment was to visit another

town and meet with the local tourist officials for an educational session. It proved to be more of an education for me than I think it was for the officials.

At the appointed time, I was picked up at the hotel and taken to their offices in the city. Six gentlemen were in the room, and we exchanged pleasantries as tea was served from a silver pot. All very posh and proper, and I was impressed with the decorations.

Everywhere you go in India, these very hospitable people offer you tea. I drank copious amounts every day, and my visits to the bathroom increased commensurately.

I sensed that the social part of the meeting was coming to a close and that the official segment was about to begin. I was in the incipient stages of a buildup in my bladder and deemed it expedient to go to the toilet then and not interrupt our meeting at a time when it would be getting interesting.

I asked if I might use their rest room.

"You are tired?" they asked.

"No, no, your washroom," I countered.

The senior official slapped his hands together twice, one of his staff entered and an order was issued in Hindi.

"Just one moment," he smiled, "It will be brought immediately."

Brought? I had visions of the office boy

bringing in a portable toilet which I would be expected to use in the presence of everyone in the room.

*   *   *

My discomfort increased as I waited for the potty to be brought in and I pondered just how I should handle this delicate situation.

There was a knock at the door and the staffer entered with a tray full of washcloths exuding a very pleasant fragrance.

He offered me one first, then the others, who wiped their necks, daubed their faces and rubbed their hands.

"I apologize for confusing you," I stammered. "I meant that I wish to use the toilet."

They talked excitedly in Hindi, then one said: "You wish to leak?"

It took all I had to suppress my laughter because by now the whole scene was getting to me, and the word "leak" somehow didn't fit the occasion or the pompous atmosphere.

"Yes," I said, "your Indian teas are so delicious, I find it difficult to stop at one cup."

No smiles.

"Ah, how nice," the leader commented. He slapped his hands together again and the same young boy entered. His boss opened a desk drawer and took out a ponderous key, one that looked like the kind used to open the front door of an enormous mansion or perhaps a castle.

"Please follow the boy," the leader said. "He will take you to a place where you can leak."

I almost laughed in his face, but I followed the young man. We descended two flights of stairs to the street, walked two blocks, turned and covered one more block before entering an archway.

We ascended one flight of stairs and arrived at a door. The youngster put the key in the lock and turned it with a great deal of effort. He pulled the door open and motioned with his hand for me to enter.

The odor inside would have stunned an elephant at 50 feet. When I completed my function, I attempted to flush it by pulling a chain that hung from a cistern over the bowl.

The chain came away in my hand. I looked for a washbowl (I think my brain had become numb from the odor!) but did not see one.

As I exited, the boy locked the door with even more difficulty than he had opened it and withdrew the heavy key. We returned to the meeting. In all, it took about 10 minutes.

*   *   *

I was greeted with smiles, and as we

attempted to turn to business, I couldn't resist asking the question, "Do you have to go all that way when you want to use the toilet?"

"Oh, no" the official said. "We use a wall downstairs."

I didn't have the nerve to ask him what they did if nature's other call had to be answered.

The Gentlemanly
Vice President

In the earlier days of incentive travel, there was less competition than there is today. The few incentive companies then operating were frequently so busy that everyone in the office, no matter what his title or duties, was called on to serve as a trip director.

Jim Gordon was vice president of our company, and, in fact, was the one who hired me into the incentive business. He was an enormous man of gentle habits and great intelligence. Despite his great weight, Jim was remarkably light on his feet, and was blessed with lots of energy.

One day, he was asked by the Director of Operations, who was responsible for assigning trip directors, if he could accompany a trip to Rome. Although his own schedule was pressing, Jim knew that other office-bound people were being pushed into service as trip directors too, so he accepted.

One of the many fine qualities Jim possessed was his genuine willingness to help people in distress. If someone's arms were full, he would either offer to carry some of the load or hold doors and elevators to help the harried individual.

The group to which he was assigned consisted of appliance dealers, and they were being transported to the Eternal City from New York by Pan American charter.

On arrival at Rome's Leonardo da Vinci Airport, the group waited for the bags to come off the airplane. One couple had obviously brought more clothing and luggage than they required, a common occurrence on incentive trips.

The airport porters were on strike, so all members of the group had to claim their own luggage, load it on carts (if they could find them), and proceed through customs.

Most customs officers in foreign countries

are not strict with incoming tourists, particularly Americans, but occasionally they will stop a couple and give their bags a perfunctory look before passing them through.

The dealer with the excess luggage couldn't find a cart, and he and his wife were trying to carry bags under their arms while holding others in their hands. Jim, ever the gallant one, offered his help and it was accepted. The couple asked him to carry one bag that was so swollen at the seams, it appeared that it would explode at any minute.

*   *   *

Jim and the couple walked past customs in the green channel, indicating they had nothing to declare. The couple preceded Jim by a few feet and sailed through, but the officer must have been curious about the case that looked ready to split its seams. He waved Jim over to a counter and asked him to open his luggage.

Jim tried to explain that the bag was not his, but the Italian officer's knowledge of English was far from perfect.

He made a motion to open the fat case. Jim politely tried to tell the officer that it would not be right for him to open another person's bag. However, despite his protestations, he had no choice but to snap the catches. The top flew open and clothing and other articles spewed all over the inspector's desk.

One particularly large cardboard box fell to the floor as other members of the group were passing. The box sprang open when it hit the ground, and condoms and other sex-related articles spilled all over. Jim reached to pick them up and his face reddened as giggles and laughter filled the air.

"This bag is not mine, really," he explained to the guests as he gathered up the items. "I'm just carrying this bag for one of the group. Really, it's not mine."

"If you're selling them, I'd like a dozen," one of the guests said as he and his wife passed, laughing so hard it drew attention to Jim's plight.

"You're supposed to be *working* on this trip, you know," another said.

"Hey, how about a dozen of those funny-looking ones in the different colors," a disembodied voice shouted from the rear.

By this time, the inspector, who had started laughing, bellowed something in Italian and two other officers came over to look.

* * *

Of course, Jim didn't reveal which couple

owned the case; that would not be proper, and
Jim was too much of a gentleman. Throughout the trip, he was the object of jokes, teas-
ing and every kind of smart remark.

He swore he would never help anyone with
luggage again.

"Elephant Balls"

Sean Kelly was an airline representative, but disappointed with the amount of traveling he was doing in his job. In fact, he had been with the airline over a year and in all that time had made only one short trip to Los Angeles.

He applied to our company for a job as a trip director. I was in charge of this department, and one of our transportation agents, who knew Sean from his visits to our office to discuss the airline he worked for, asked if I would interview him.

The best way to describe Sean is to com-
pare him to a gorilla. He stood 6'4", weighed
about 240 pounds and resembled an All-Pro
tackle. He had a pleasant if boisterous personality and was obviously gregarious.
Moreover, he was energetic and intelligent and
looked like he would be a good worker. So I
hired him.

Maybe it was due to his height and weight,
but Sean had a peculiar gait and walked
almost as if he were bowlegged. He waddled
rather than walked.

He had been with us only two days when
one of the other trip directors observed him
moving and said, "Sean, you walk as though
you had elephant balls." And so Sean
acquired a nickname. Soon everybody called
him by the initials of this physical affliction,
and he became known as "E.B.," which devel-
oped into the easier-to-pronounce "Eby."

I kept copious notes of the incidents,
humorous and otherwise, that occurred during my career, yet nowhere could I find Eby's
own name. I had to call numerous friends I
had worked with in earlier years before finding
someone who remembered that Eby's first
name was Sean.

It is normal in our business to give new
hires on-the-job training. They go along as a
"fifth wheel" so that a client who has been

promised one "experienced, professionally trained trip director for every 50 guests" is given this number. The trainee is assigned as additional travel staff.

We had a charter to Barbados coming up, and I had scheduled myself as the trip director. At that particular time, our company had a lot of business in Barbados, and I scheduled myself to go two days in advance of the group rather than the normal one. This was due to the fact that I had planned meetings with hotel and tourist officials and wanted to complete these before the group arrived.

Another trip director who would be serving on the program, Tom Grimsby, asked if it would be helpful for him to accompany me. As there was quite a bit of work to be done, I thought that it would indeed be beneficial for him to travel with me. So we flew to Barbados together.

I assigned Eby to the program, and advised him to come down the day before the charter so Tom and I could show him a little of the island.

We arrived late in the evening at the hotel in Barbados and were assigned a twin, as was the policy of our company. Today, incentive houses tend to give the trip director and staff single rooms, but this was not the case in the '60s when this incident took place.

The next morning, as we were having breakfast prior to setting off for our first meeting, I heard a familiar voice cry out: "Peter, what are you doing here so early? I thought you were arriving tonight." It was Miriam Henderson, the hotel's front office manager.

I explained our change of plans to Miriam, who then told me she had a suite for me. "A suite?" I cried, astonished. "Why should I be given a suite?"

"You're very important to our hotel," she responded. "You give us lots of business and we want to treat you right." I protested that I was only a trip director, not a VIP, but Miriam insisted.

Suddenly, it dawned on me why she was being so persistent in having me take the suite. I recalled some of our trip directors and others with our competition mentioning that Miriam was a nymphomaniac and that she always gave the trip director a suite. Later in the evening, she would let herself into the suite with a passkey and jump into bed with her luckless victim. I say luckless because Miriam, as nice a woman as she was, lacked the physical attributes necessary to help the average man attain the required symptom of extreme passion.

I had known Miriam for some time, but had never been the trip director of a group program in her hotel, hence my slow reaction to her generous offer.

I was in such a hurry to finish breakfast and then head for my meeting in town that I agreed to take the suite and thanked her for her generosity.

We concluded our business appointments in the city, then Tom and I drove out to the airport to pick up Eby. En route, I burst into a paroxysm of laughter. Tom asked the reason for my hilarity and I let him in on a plan that was evolving in my mind.

"Let's give Eby the suite," I said. Tom, who was well aware of Miriam's idiosyncrasies, laughed with me. We must have caused a few heads to turn as we parked the car at the airport, both laughing like idiots.

We took Eby back to the hotel, and I whispered to Adam, the clerk at the front desk, that he should give the suite to Eby.

"But the suite is for you," he remonstrated. "Miriam gave me strict instructions."

I assured him that I would clear it with her, and not to worry. And so Tom and a bellboy and I took Eby to his luxurious accommodations.

When Eby saw the suite, his jaw dropped. "You mean this suite is just for us?"

"Us?" Tom bellowed. "This suite is for you. Each of us gets a suite. We give this hotel millions of dollars of business and they treat us right. All trip directors get suites."

Eby couldn't believe his good fortune. During dinner that night, he brought it up two or three times, and we told him he would just have to get used to it.

We returned to the hotel around midnight, having shown Eby several other properties and restaurants. As we bade each other good night, I reminded him to meet Tom and me at 8:00 o'clock for breakfast so we would have time to set up the hospitality desk and check out those last-minute details that required attention before the group arrived.

Next morning, Tom and I were seated at the breakfast table awaiting Eby. "Here he comes," Tom said. We tried to act nonchalant as Eby swung his leg over a chair, much as a horseman mounts his steed.

Slamming his fist down on the table so powerfully that the silverware jumped, he blurted out, "You guys will never believe this, but..."

*   *   *

An interesting footnote to this story occurred about three weeks later when one of the senior trip directors came into my office and asked: "Who hired Eby? This guy's got

problems."

I asked what he meant, and he revealed that, on a program to Jamaica right after the Barbados trip, Eby complained about somebody playing a trick on him by not giving him a suite but instead putting him in an ordinary twin room with another trip director.

Lunch With Nobility

Down through the years, I've traveled with just about every type of client, and mostly they could be categorized as humorous and gregarious.

There is one client with whom I have traveled frequently on inspection trips who has an abundance of both qualities. This particular client and I had gone to Tobago, a beautiful little island deep down in the Caribbean, to check it out for his group.

We attended the manager's cocktail party

in the hotel on our first evening in Tobago and were introduced to two elderly titled ladies from England who were vacationing. One was Lady Skippington, the other Lady Hargreaves.

Their proper English accents required us to be very attentive to what they were saying so that we could understand them. During our polite conversation, Lady Skippington mentioned that she was having a most enjoyable vacation but that she had been unable to bathe (not swim, mind you!) in the ocean because the waves had been rather rough of late and she was very frail.

My client, Frank Beaumont, told her that we were taking a cruise to the famous Buccoo Reef the next morning, ending up at the island's gorgeous beach, Pigeon Point.

Frank suggested that they meet us there and, if the sea was rough, he would carry Lady Skippington into the sea so that she would not be bowled over.

She was overjoyed and assured Frank that she and Lady Hargreaves would be there the next day at noon. The hotel manager, who was listening to the conversation, offered to provide the lunch at the beach, which was readily accepted.

After our visit to the reef the next morning, our glass-bottom boat dropped us off at Pigeon Point about 11:30 A.M.

Not only is Frank a client of great and enjoyable humor, he genuinely likes people and easily engages in conversation with those around him.

As we strolled the beach awaiting the arrival of the ladies-in-waiting and lunch, we stopped under a thatched umbrella to escape the hot sun and enjoy a cool drink.

A young man and woman were already under the umbrella, and Frank opened up the conversation by introducing himself and me.

The young couple, it turned out, were medical students from London who were serving a six-month internship at St. George Hospital in Tobago.

The conversation turned to their stay on this idyllic island, and both agreed it was a paradise but mentioned that they were paid such a meager salary that they were unable to dine anywhere but at the hospital. They commented that the food at this particular hospital was bland and uninteresting.

"Well, then," said Frank, now tremendously enjoying himself, "would you like to join us for lunch?" He went on to tell them that we were having lunch catered on the beach and that two ladies-in-waiting to the Queen would be joining us.

Consider the situation: If you had just met two men on a quiet beach on a small island that most people have never heard of and they invited you to have lunch with them and two titled English ladies, with neither lunch nor ladies in sight, what would have been your reaction?

Well, that's the reaction we got from the medical students, who must have wondered what sort of game we were playing. They murmured their acceptance, smiling all the while as if thinking to themselves that the best way to handle these two oddballs was to humor them.

We chatted for about another half-an-hour until the time reached 12:20 P.M. and the students, appearing restless, said that they really should be getting back to the hospital. They rose and extended their hands to say goodbye when suddenly three vans came into view.

From the first stepped the manager and the two ladies. From the other two came tables, huge boxes of food and musical instruments.

Lady Skippington, Lady Hargreaves and the manager were introduced to the interns while white linen cloths were spread over the tables, which were then adorned with silverware, flowers, plates and numerous condiments.

Meanwhile, a chef, resplendent in his white uniform and tall hat, set about preparing the

coals on a grill. I'm certain that Pigeon Point beach never saw anything like it.

The hotel's eight-member steel band began to play as the salads, rolls and desserts were arranged on the table along with crystal glasses and candelabra. There were even candles in the candelabra, but only for show—the breeze would have made it impossible for them to stay lit.

*   *   *

As the chef readied the steaks and fish, the students' faces reflected complete bewilderment. Was this real? They must have thought they were hallucinating.

The steaks were served and, during the meal, the ladies-in-waiting regaled us with stories of royal encounters.

One of the students asked Lady Skippington if she saw the Queen many times during the year.

"Of course, my dear," she answered. "I have to attend many royal functions as a lady-in-waiting and curtsey to Her Majesty."

Later, Frank and I agreed that if Lady Skippington, being as fragile as she was, had curtsied to the Queen, Prince Philip must have had to give her a hand to get back up.

Then Frank made good on his promise to

Lady Skippington. They strolled to the water's edge and he carried her in his arms a few feet from the shore, where she spent several minutes soaking in the warm waters of the Caribbean.

Soon it was time for good-byes and, as the vans were loaded to return to the hotel, Lady Skippington and Lady Hargreaves wished the medical students a happy stay in Tobago.

We, too, bade them farewell, but the astonished looks on their faces convinced us that they had still not resolved the question:

"Is this real?"

The Cremation

It is considered a violation of the incentive industry's ethics to propose to a client a destination that has not been checked out.

Consequently, I was given the assignment to fly to a fabled island in Southeast Asia to assess its potential for incentive groups. Our company planned to recommend the island to an automotive account, but first we had to ascertain that the destination would meet all our criteria by having someone from the office give his imprimatur.

On arrival at the island's airport, I was met by a representative of the travel company we had appointed as our land agent, a very attractive woman who was accompanied by the manager of the hotel where I would be staying and whose property we would use in the program.

As we drove to the hotel, Lani, our agent, said, "We have a wonderful surprise for you."

"Should we tell him?" she asked the hotelier.

The manager said, "No, let's keep him in suspense."

My curiosity was piqued, and I suggested that they tell me so I could also enjoy the anticipation. They were adamant; I would be told the evening before the surprise would materialize.

All sorts of wonderful (and salacious) thoughts filled my mind. As it turned out, none of my reveries came even close to the mark.

The surprise was to be revealed to me in two days, and I was now becoming so consumed with what it might be that I'm sure I missed some of the more important points of the island that I should have included in my report.

I can't remember ever being so filled with curiosity and excitement as I was at that time, waiting to have this surprise unfold. Lani must have mentioned it six or seven times over the next two days with the assurance that I was going to be very pleased indeed.

She joined the manager and me for dinner in the hotel on the evening of the disclosure. The assistant manager, Martin Wong, whom I had met several times before in our offices and at meetings abroad, also dined with us.

(Incidentally, it is a common practice with Asian businessmen to give themselves a Westernized first name that is easier for clients to remember and pronounce.)

*   *   *

I wolfed down the meal in the hope that I might speed up the proceedings and thus learn more quickly whether I was going to have a dozen nubile maidens in my room that evening or be given a precious jewel from the government as a memento of my visit.

The moment arrived. Lani suggested that the manager be the one to tell me.

"No," he said gallantly (but irritating me with the delay), "I think that, as the only woman at our table, you should be given the honor."

She was pleased. You could tell by the smile that creased her face. "Oh, thank you. That's very kind of you." She was genuinely touched that he would allow her to be center stage.

"Oh, get on with it," I thought to myself. "Just tell me whether it's a dozen maidens or six. Even one will do."

"Are you ready?" she asked. I had been ready—in agony almost—since she first mentioned it on my arrival. I really thought she was going to say, "Close your eyes now."

"Tomorrow, after lunch," she began, obviously relishing the telling of it because she was speaking so slowly, "you are going to be honored by our government ('It's the jewel!' I thought) with a cremation."

"A what?" I blurted out, momentarily stunned.

"A cremation," she replied.

"A cremation? Cremation of what?"

"Not what," she corrected me, still smiling, "whom."

"I don't understand," I continued, wondering if they planned to roast those nubile maidens.

"Let me explain," she said. "On our island, when an important personage visits us, we recognize his importance by having him as the honored guest at a cremation. That is, of course, if there is a corpse to be cremated.

"You are being especially honored by presiding at a cremation of a very distinguished legislator who died two days before your arrival. He should have been cremated the day you came to our island, but we held him over [so help me, those were her exact words] so that you could sit in the High Guest's Chair."

I learned later that, on this particular

island, it is indeed a great honor to sit in the High Guest's Chair at a cremation. The greater the stature of the deceased, the greater the honor accorded the guest. As the dead man had been a state legislator, the honor could only have been higher if the corpse had been that of the president or a member of his cabinet.

This was my hosts' way of recognizing the importance of my visit that would, if I found the destination satisfactory, result in many groups of Americans being brought to their island.

When Lani disclosed that they had "held him over" just for me, I indecorously (or maybe it was nervously) shouted, "Oh, don't hold him over just for me; burn him, burn him tonight."

I was assured everything was in readiness and that the next day after lunch (can you imagine it, "after lunch"?) I would be taken to the cremation grounds.

Martin, more knowledgable of our western ways, filled me in on the details when we were alone. He explained what I should do and gave me courage by saying that he and Lani would join me on seats flanking the High Guest's Chair and advise me what to do.

I did not sleep well that night. Normally, I don't like to go to funerals and I force myself to attend them only out of respect for the deceased. But a cremation!

A sightseeing tour was arranged the following morning, ending at a lovely hillside restaurant where a truly magnificent buffet lunch
lay in readiness. I poked at a piece of melon;
my stomach was not in the mood for the delicious food.

Lani asked if I was excited about the cremation and, when I told her that was an
understatement, I know she misinterpreted
my meaning. "Oh, wonderful! I'm so happy,"
she exclaimed.

Next our driver came over to me at the table
and whispered in my ear, "Just another hour
or so and we'll be leaving for the cremation
grounds. Don't worry, the time will pass quickly and we'll soon be there." It was as though
we were all going to a Frank Sinatra concert.

Three others, a man and two women,
whom I had not met or seen before, stopped at
our table, bowed to me, smiled and said, "We'll
be at the cremation." Everybody in the restaurant knew that I would be in the High Guest's
Chair. What they didn't know was that I wondered if I would be less enthusiastic going to
the electric chair.

Lunch over, we drove to the cremation
grounds. I thought they should have been
called the Bedlam Grounds. Police were
directing traffic in the huge crowd, but our car

was waved through quickly. So this is how the rich and famous live, I thought.

I was led to the High Guest's Chair. It was covered with flowers of every color of the rainbow, a spectacular sight. The two chairs flanking it were unadorned.

As I sat down, I noticed that there were even flowers on the seat of my chair and that they would be crushed when I descended.

The crowd was not only composed of locals; there were close to ten tour buses, and I heard German and French spoken. Martin mentioned that there were also tourists from Scandinavia, Italy, Australia and Hong Kong.

Everyone looked at me as if I were a god. "Why would tourists come to a cremation" I thought to myself, "when they could be sunning themselves on the island's beautiful beaches or shopping in town?"

Trying to maintain an air of dignity, I looked around the grounds and noticed that there was a stone statue of a cow atop a nearby concrete platform.

Martin pointed out that the corpse would be taken to the statue and that the upper half of the cow would be removed and the body placed inside. The cow's belly had wires strung across it to permit the flames to consume the body.

Martin now told me what was expected of me and what my functions would be.

Music suddenly filled the air, and from somewhere in the crowd appeared six brown-skinned little men playing reed instruments. They slowly walked to the High Guest's Chair and bowed to me.

I returned their obeisances with a perfunctory nod (the guest has to act important!). They vanished in the crowd to return a few minutes later playing more incomprehensible music.

This time, however, they were leading six pallbearers carrying a stretcher with a body under a white shroud. The top of the legislator's white-maned head and bare feet extruded from opposite ends of the sheet.

The procession stopped in front of me. They raised the stretcher so that I could have a better view, but did not remove the shroud. I wondered if I was supposed to bless the covered corpse.

The musicians and bearers respectfully bowed to me, and I nodded in return.

Then they proceeded to the statue, removed the upper half of the cow and placed the body inside. Thick logs of wood had now been placed underneath as well as several old tires. Gasoline was poured on the materials.

One of the pallbearers lighted a torch and quickly walked over to me, holding it aloft. He bowed and then extended it to me.

Martin told me that I had a choice. I could

accept the torch and ignite the pyre or nod to the pallbearer, who would interpret my nod to mean that I preferred him to do his own dirty work. I nodded to him.

He threw the torch on the pyre and the flames exploded as shreds of white cloth dropped from the cow's belly onto the fire.

I have always been cognizant of the fact that, when traveling abroad, I am an ambassador of the U.S. I have been careful not to offend foreigners and hopefully to reflect a proper image. I would have stayed until the flames died out if that was what was expected of me, but Michael assured me I could leave after the fire was lit and that this would be considered proper behavior. I waited five minutes more and then departed.

As we moved to our car, my impression that I was regarded as something approaching deity was reinforced as the crowd stepped back to create a path for me—much like the parting of the Red Sea.

Comfortably seated in the car, Lani asked me if I was "proud and pleased."

"I don't think I have ever been so honored as I was today," I responded.

She smiled, obviously gratified.

I didn't have the heart to tell her I would have preferred the dozen nubile maidens.

The Sheep's Eye

There is no question that those who are employed in the incentive business, particularly the travel end of it, lead glamorous lives. They get to see the world, and usually in a first-class way.

But sometimes it can be very hard and tiring work. Trip directors may work as many as 16 hours a day, while some go halfway around the world and don't even have a chance to venture out of the hotel or see anything of the country.

On occasion, there have been embarrassing situations, good examples of which have been recounted elsewhere in this book.

And there have been incidents in which people have had to do things they would much rather not have done. One such incident happened to me on a fam trip to Cairo, Egypt.

There were 12 of us from different incentive companies who had been invited to visit Egypt so that we could be exposed to the incredible wonders of that extraordinary country.

One evening, as a special treat, we were to dine with a sheik in his tent in the desert. Sheiks have regular city residences, of course, but some do maintain desert homes where they retreat on occasion to escape the tribulations of modern society.

This particular tent was about 20 miles from Cairo, and we were transported in Land Rovers over roads and sand dunes to the oasis where it was situated.

I will never forget the beauty of the desert as it glistened under a star-filled sky illuminated by the brightest moon I think I have ever seen.

When we arrived at the tent, we were seated on plush, comfortable cushions and served non-alcoholic refreshments and sweetmeats as beautiful belly dancers gyrated before us.

The meal was delicious and consisted of many courses. None of us knew what we were being served, and one wise fellow traveler suggested that we should enjoy the food and stifle our curiosity.

Midway through the banquet, the sheik clapped his hands together and the belly dancers gave their stomach muscles a rest.

The musicians switched the tempo of their music from fast to slow as ornately attired young boys entered carrying velvet cushions on which rested silver bowls. Floating in each bowl was a cabbage-like leaf holding — a sheep's eye.

A bowl was placed before each guest. I looked at the eye and it looked at me.

I was seated next to one of several Egyptian travel agents who had accompanied us on this safari. As I have indicated in another chapter, I have always been conscious that I represent my country when I am abroad and conduct myself accordingly.

I asked the travel agent seated beside me if we were required to eat the eye.

"Oh, my goodness, yes," he replied enthusiastically. "They are a delicacy, you know. You will enjoy it, I promise you." Saying that, he delicately lifted the eye with his left index finger, middle finger and thumb and placed it in his mouth with a heavenly expression on his face.

I have eaten strange foods around the world and have enjoyed most of them. I have seldom been reluctant to try unusual foods; I am not squeamish. At least, I didn't think I was a fastidious eater until I entered into a staring match with the sheep's eye.

"Would it offend anyone if I didn't eat it?" I asked my companion. "I would not wish to offend our host, but I'm afraid that eating a sheep's eye is not my idea of epicurean dining."

"Oh, my friend, I'm afraid the sheik has taken great pains to grace his table with this rare delicacy. I think he would be upset if you did not eat it. He may feel you disapprove of his choice of menu which was especially prepared to honor you and your friends."

He told me that if I was reluctant to eat the eye that there was an easy way to please everyone. "You do not need to chew it," he said. "I suggest you swallow it. You see, the eye is very moist and will slide down your throat like an oyster."

His very description almost made me sick, a most unusual condition for me. I mustered every ounce of courage I had and lifted the squishy optic in my left hand, in the approved fashion, and popped it in my mouth.

Try as I might, my throat fought my efforts. I couldn't swallow it and gagged for fully 30 seconds before it went down.

For a few minutes afterwards, I didn't know if I would have to excuse myself and regurgitate outside the tent. To this day, I still get a funny feeling in my stomach when I think of that sheep's eye, and the sensation is made even more acute by writing about it.

When the function ended, we reboarded our Land Rovers to return to our hotel in Cairo. There were six of my fellow travelers in the vehicle as we sped over the dunes.

"What did you think of that eye?" I asked them. "I almost choked and thought I would be sick."

In unison, they replied, "Are you kidding? I wouldn't eat that crap!"

So much for my ambassadorial sentiments, I thought.

Eastern Europe

There was little that was humorous about traveling in the Soviet Union or its satellites before the advent of glasnost and perestroika. There were incidents, however, that occurred in my travels throughout eastern Europe that may be deemed more interesting than laugh-provoking, but humor did manage to raise its head every so often.

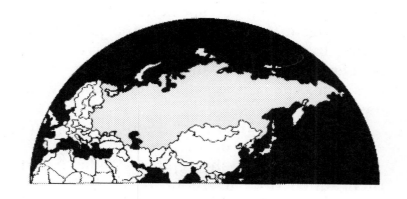

I. My Detention

On my first trip to Russia back in 1967, I stepped off the plane to be informed by a gruff-looking military man that my visa was incorrect. Actually, he spoke no English and I had to find an agent of Intourist, the government-owned tourist agency in the Soviet Union, to translate. I thought it strange that an immigration officer could speak no English. English has become the universal language and, if you are employed in a position that brings you in contact with tourists, it is mandatory that you speak it.

The agent informed me that the soldier had stated that my document was incorrect. The soldier said my visa showed the date of my arrival as late in the evening of the following day.

I asked the Intourist agent if she was expecting me today or tomorrow.

Unhesitatingly, she replied, "Today," and then added that my room at the hotel and transportation were both scheduled for arrival that day, too. The agent, somewhat embarrassed, said that the soldier told her to tell me that the American embassy had put the wrong date on my visa.

She was embarrassed because she knew that a visa to enter the Soviet Union, or any country for that matter, must be issued by the embassy or consulate of the country being visited. I could see the futility of arguing, so I asked her what my alternative was.

The agent mentioned that I would have to be detained at the "airport hotel" (I have placed that in quotation marks for a reason I'll explain later) for the night and they would straighten out the matter of my visa in the morning.

The soldier told me (no, he *warned* me) that I was technically in the Soviet Union illegally and that I was not to step outside the hotel until the following morning, at which time I was to come straight across the road to the airport and report to the Intourist office.

It was not quite the welcome I had hoped for, but somehow I was not overly surprised. I was escorted across the road to the hotel.

It was not a hotel, but a military barracks. The following morning, I saw soldiers on parade outside my window, doing drills and quick-time marches.

The room I was assigned had no toilet ("it's down the hallway") and there were no shower or bath facilities. It had one small bed and a chest of drawers. A naked light bulb hung by a long cord from the high ceiling.

A machine-gun toting soldier paced outside my room all night (I know because I didn't sleep too well and could hear him with his jackboots noisily walking the floor).

The next morning, I rose, put on the same clothes I had been wearing for the last two days and, armed with a three days' growth of beard which made me look very unkempt, headed for the airport across the street.

As I left the room, the soldier was talking to a man who addressed me in Russian. I shrugged my shoulders, asked him if he spoke English or French, and gave him an opportunity to shrug his shoulders.

As I walked away, he vehemently demanded

something of me while the soldier stood like a dummy with his gun held to his chest, staring at me.

I waved my hand indicating I was unable to communicate with him and said, "Airport," hoping that the English pronunciation was close enough to the Russian that he might understand where I was going. (I later learned he wanted a voucher from me for my stay. I thought it should have been the other way around!)

I reported to the Intourist office, and a representative told me to have a cup of tea or coffee and report back in about two hours. I was again warned not to leave the airport grounds, as it would be considered a very serious offense.

(At the time of this incident, there was only one international airport in Moscow, which was known as Sheremeteyevo Airport #1. Now there are two. The second is known by the imaginative name of Sheremeteyevo Airport #2.)

I walked over to a small bar on the main floor and tried some tea, which I found surprisingly good. Bored, I walked upstairs to the observation gallery and watched planes land and take off. Tiring of people waving to friends below about to board aircraft for parts unknown, I took a look inside a restaurant adjacent to the waving gallery.

I returned to the snack bar and tried another cup of tea. As I sipped it, workmen began rolling out a red carpet and putting out cordoned poles on either side of it. Television cameras were wheeled into position, and newspaper photographers found vantage points from which they could shoot pictures.

Several large black limousines stopped at the front door of the airport, and numerous dignitaries emerged before moving ahead to the red carpet. As they passed, I slipped into the line, assuming they were headed for the restaurant at the top of the stairs. But when they reached the top of the stairway, they turned left into a private room. I tried to separate from them but was almost pushed into the room.

It was arranged for lunch and the tables had been pushed together to form one huge "U." I seated myself and, almost immediately, someone at the head table rose, said a few words which I assumed were a toast, raised his glass of vodka and downed it in one gulp.

I have been a lifelong teetotaler simply because I have never enjoyed the taste of alcohol, so I left my vodka untouched.

The fellow on my right spoke to me while motioning with his hand to my glass of vodka. I went through the same motions as with the "hotel" manager.

"I'm sorry, I don't speak Russian. Do you speak English or French?"

He looked at me strangely, shook his head and said, "Nyet." He pointed to my full glass, and I didn't need to speak Russian to know what he meant. I handed it to him and he smiled.

By this time, the fellow on my left, who was watching all of this, had decided that it was yet another example of an American treating a Russian — him! — unfairly and that he would act more quickly next time and grab the vodka.

The waiters filled the glasses for the second toast. This time, the fellow on my left grabbed my glass in his right hand, swallowed his drink in his left hand and then followed that with mine.

Throughout the lunch, it became a contest as to which of the two would grab my glass first. They didn't ask; they just helped themselves.

I didn't mind. I knew very well I shouldn't have been there in the first place and was happy to keep them from asking too many questions.

During the toasts, a television camera on a dolly moved up the middle of the "U" taking footage, obviously for that evening's newscast.

Photographers were allowed into the room

to take some shots, and I complied by raising my empty glass and smiling, more out of fear than enjoyment.

After lunch, there were several speeches; then it was time to leave. We moved out through another door on the far side of the room and down some stairs. I saw an open door at the bottom and looked beyond to see that it led outside to the tarmac. To my horror, I realized the group was going out to an airplane!

By this time, I was becoming very uncomfortable. I knew I couldn't walk out to the tarmac. I would be arrested for sure because I knew that I was now in a restricted area and in violation of the ban that had been placed on me.

There was a soldier at the bottom of the steps, a machine gun in his hands. When the group descended, they turned right. I turned left to head back into the terminal, withdrew my American passport from inside my coat pocket and shouted *"do svidania"* (good-bye) to my erstwhile companions.

They were so full of vodka they couldn't have cared less where I was going. They shouted *"do svidania"* in return and walked on.

I waved my American passport at the soldier and passed him. He turned and looked at me, uncertain as to whether to challenge me or let me go. I am sure that, because I had been with this distinguished group, he thought I must be important and let me continue.

I moved along the hallway, went though another door and, thank God, found myself in the main terminal. I was headed back to the snack bar when I heard a voice call my name.

"Where have you been?" the Intourist agent asked. "We have been looking all over for you."

"I have been up in the waving gallery, in the snack bar, in the men's room, walking up and down the terminal, anything to fight the boredom," I growled. "Where else could I go? You made it very clear that I was not to leave the airport."

My reply obviously satisfied him, and he said, "Your visa has been approved. You can now go into Moscow."

The next day I saw photos of my luncheon companions in the newspaper exchanging toasts. My picture, thankfully, was not among them.

The reason the dignitaries had gathered for lunch, gone out onto the tarmac and boarded a plane was explained in the newspaper article, which I had someone translate for me.

It was the inaugural flight of the Soviet airline, Aeroflot, from Moscow to New York!

2. The Student

I really don't know why I found the incident, on which this story is based, so funny. In cold print it may not carry the same punch. I only know that when I listened to one of our travel staff sadly relate the details, I laughed uncontrollably.

We had a group in Leningrad and, during and after dinner, there was music for dancing. The band had 12 musicians, and they played very well; in fact, they were great. Then we realized why they were so delightful to listen to: they were playing American music to American arrangements.

The dance floor, though large, filled rapidly, and soon the place was swinging as if we were in Detroit or Kansas City.

During an intermission, members of our group spoke with some of the musicians. They explained that they had recordings of Glenn Miller, Tommy Dorsey and other great American bandsmen. They faithfully copied the styles. and their rhythms showed how well they had practiced.

One musician said, with more than a tinge of sadness, that he had a brother, also a musician, who lived "somewhere in California." He asked question after question about America with an intense interest until it was time to return to the platform and resume his place in the band.

*　　*　　*

At that time, the major hotels in the Soviet Union were for foreigners only. No Soviets or vacationers from other Communist countries were allowed to stay in these facilities. In fact, no people from the satellites were even permitted inside for a drink in the bar or a cup of coffee in a restaurant.

Guards in military as well as civilian garb

were stationed at desks near the front door and challenged anyone who did not appear to be Western. The trick was the clothing, with foreign apparel being so far superior to anything obtainable in the Eastern Bloc countries as to make the visitor stand out.

*   *   *

While our group was enjoying the dancing with other foreign guests, one of our travel staff, Darrell Alexander, with whom I shared a room, engaged in conversation with some girls at the next table.

Darrell was off duty and so on his own time. One of the girls told him she was a Romanian studying at the University of Leningrad. She had boldly entered the hotel and managed to sneak past the guard. She joined a table of tourists who invited her to have a drink with them.

The student mentioned to Darrell that, if he could find a bottle of champagne, he could accompany her back to the dorm at the university and meet some other students.

He readily accepted the offer, ordered a bottle of champagne and, as he passed me, said, "I'm going to university, hopefully for an education. Don't wait up for me and don't be worried if I don't come home tonight." He winked and was gone.

Shortly afterwards, I went up to our room and prepared for bed. I was brushing my teeth when I heard a key in the lock and in walked Darrell.

"Must've been a helluva party," I muttered, surprised to see him.

A smile crept across his face. "What a country. Melanka [the student's name] and I left the hotel and got about ten yards from the front door when a big, black car drove up.

"Two guys with leather coats down to their ankles and straight out of a 'B' movie got out and called something in Russian, and Melanka said, 'We must stop.'

"The characters flashed identification and talked back and forth with her for a few minutes. Of course, I couldn't understand what they were talking about. Then Melanka turns to me and says, 'I'm sorry, but I must go with my friends.' They escorted her to their car and drove off, leaving me like an uninvited guest at a wedding."

Then he started to laugh. "Can you believe it?"

Maybe it was the look on Darrell's face; maybe it was the way he told the story; maybe it was the way his features reflected the disappointment of losing a great prospect; or maybe it was all of the above, but I began to laugh.

"What a strange country this is," he continued to mumble. "Can you believe it?"

"Shit," he said, and turned on the shower.

3. The Arrogant Pilot

Before World War II, Budapest was known as one of the "Queen" cities of Europe. There were no more than a dozen such cities, among them London, Edinburgh, Paris, Rome, Prague, Vienna, Leningrad and Budapest, to name most of them.

Each earned its title because of the beauty of its architecture, the classic design of its layout and its numerous eye-pleasing parks and gardens.

Budapest was, at one time, two cities—

Buda and Pest — separated by the River Danube. Buda was built on a hill while Pest was flat, and, in 1873, they incorporated as one city.

I had been invited to visit this remarkably beautiful metropolis in 1978 and had marveled at the comparative openness in terms of civil freedoms. It was the most vibrant of all eastern European cities, and its people seemed friendlier and much less oppressed than those in the other satellite nations.

I was graciously shown the city's hotels, spas, restaurants and nightclubs (of which Budapest has many) and then taken on tours into the country. The government wanted me to see what Hungary had to offer in the hope that my report would be favorable and influence my company to bring incentive groups. I quickly formed the opinion that visitors couldn't fail to be awed by Hungary's capital city.

It surprised me that the officials who showed me around relished telling anti-Soviet jokes. One, who held a high-ranking position, told me that he had been a "freedom fighter" during the Hungarian uprising in 1956.

"We waited at the top of the hill on the Buda side and watched the Russian tanks cross the bridge over the Danube. As they surged up the cobblestone street, we poured barrels of oil down the incline," he said, laughing so hard that the tears were coursing down his cheeks.

"We watched the tanks slither and lose control, then slide back down the street and into the river."

I wondered why they were so free with their tongues and why they told me so much. I know I admired their courage.

*   *   *

At the end of my trip, I boarded a Russian-built Ilyushin aircraft of the Hungarian airline, Malev, along with a government official based in Denmark who had accompanied me on my visit and was now returning to his post in Copenhagen.

Shortly before takeoff, a flight attendant came to my seat and said the captain would like to have us join him in the cockpit. We were delighted to accept.

The cockpit was one of the strangest I have ever seen. It was the one and only time I have ever been in the flight deck of a Russian-made airliner, although I have flown in most of their models.

The flight panel was remarkably flat, and the dials appeared enormous when compared to those of Western aircraft. It had far fewer instruments. The pilot's and co-pilot's controls looked as if they had been glued to the end of one-by-six boards that came straight out of the floor. It made me think of a "do-it-yourself" kit that you assemble at home.

The pilot was personable and spoke excellent English. I remarked that this was my first time in the cockpit of a Russian airliner and commented on how much the aircraft resembled a Boeing 727 (they both have three engines mounted in the tail).

The pilot's demeanor suddenly changed. "Oh, this is much better. This aircraft is far superior and is much more solidly built," he said.

"Oh, you've flown a 727, then?" I asked.

"No," he replied, "but I know this is a much better performing aircraft. I fly it several times every month."

"How can you say it's superior when you haven't flown a 727? It seems to me that you would have to have flown both aircraft to be able to make a determination as to which was the better machine."

By now, my normally polite manner was fading. I can easily become upset when foreigners mock American equipment, and this pilot was making asinine statements that had no basis in fact.

"I've seen the 727, and I've read a lot about

it, so I know it can't perform nearly as well as this aircraft."

I was readying my reply when the government official interrupted and muttered something in his own language to the pilot, who said, "You must now excuse me, please, as we have to prepare for departure."

"He's been reprimanded," I thought. "Serves him right. If I ever come back, I hope he's loading the bags on Ilyushins instead of flying them."

4. The Tipsy Official

Unless you are an oenologist, it may come as a surprise to learn that one of the finest wines in the world is made in Constanta, Romania. It is called Murfatlar.

As the country is able to produce only a limited number of bottles a year, the wine is not exported beyond the Eastern Bloc countries. This restriction may have been or soon may be lifted now that democracy is returning to the former Communist nation.

I had a client, now retired, who would willingly attest to the delicious flavors of Murfatlar wines. We were on an inspection trip to several cities on the Black Sea. My company had sold an incentive program to a tire company and the trip being offered their winning dealers and their spouses was a cruise on the Black Sea.

This was a perfect example of a specially designed program. As there were no ships sailing the Black Sea on a regular basis, we arranged to charter a vessel for the group.

Several people in our office had conceived the idea for this special cruise, and the uniqueness of the proposal was one of the reasons our company was awarded this valuable account. The trouble, however, was that, as there were no liners cruising the Black Sea on the itinerary we had devised, we had to do the inspection trip to the port cities by air.

The cruise schedule called for stops at Varna, Bulgaria; Constanta, Romania; Yalta, the Soviet Union; and Istanbul and Izmir, Turkey. The cruise was planned to begin and end in Athens, Greece.

The client, Leo Simmons, and I flew from Athens to Varna then on to Bucharest, capital of Romania. We stopped overnight in Bucharest to meet with Romanian tourist officials.

They were very pleased that we would be bringing an American incentive group (the first to visit their country) and they expressed the hope that it would be the first of many.

So enthused were the Romanians that one

of the top officials of the tourist office insisted on accompanying us to Constanta to insure that our visit was a smooth and pleasant one.

He was a small, portly man with an ebullient personality and a delightful sense of humor. Both Leo and I liked him from the moment we met him. He loved to tell jokes and had a hearty laugh.

On our flight from Bucharest to Constanta, we also learned that our friend liked to drink. He downed three glasses of a very potent plum brandy that revealed yet another talent—he loved to sing. He wasn't good, but he was loud.

The flight attendants were upset and made no attempt to disguise their contempt for his behavior. That is, until they learned who he was, and then an amazing transformation came over them. They were all smiles, and the plum brandy bottle was never out of sight.

There was one discomforting occurrence as we landed in Constanta. Three rows of fighter planes were lined up on the ground. A loud alarm sounded as we were deplaning onto the tarmac (they didn't have jetways), and suddenly the tranquillity of the scene was shattered as scores of pilots ran to their jets and roared their engines before racing down the runways. We later learned they were on an alert status because of an American action which I can't now recall.

The official was in such a jovial mood by

this time that he downplayed the maneuver as "boys with their toys."

A car and driver and local dignitaries greeted us, and we spent a few minutes together before departing. We toured Constanta (which, incidentally, has one of the largest collections of Roman ruins outside of Rome!) and reviewed its business section, world-famous health spas and other landmarks.

The last stop was at Murfatlar. The Romanians are justifiably proud of these vineyards. The winery is enclosed in a modern building made of pine wood surrounded by splendidly landscaped grounds in the middle of a forest. The interior was immaculately clean but sparsely furnished.

The guides show how the wines, brandies and liqueurs are made before directing visitors into the wine-tasting room. Here, assistants liberally pour the drinks into paper cups and provide the tasters with slices of buttered bread to cleanse the palate before switching from one wine to another.

The tourist official demonstrated an incredible capacity for alcohol, and the joviality of his mood grew commensurately with his consumption. He serenaded the assistants, who obviously knew him well and were not in the least inclined to stop pouring the samples, despite the raucousness of his singing voice which could be heard all over the building.

We had a plane to catch and so, reluctantly, we responded to our driver's reminder that it was time to go.

Shakily, Leo rose, but our Romanian friend was incapable of standing up. The driver and I took one arm each and assisted him into the car. Albeit slowly, Leo made it on his own without the need of any help.

As we headed to the airport, the driver said he thought it would be better if the official stayed overnight at a government apartment in Constanta and returned to Bucharest the next day. I had a feeling the driver had had a lot of experience driving his boss around.

The tourist official sang from the moment we left Murfatlar until we arrived at the special apartment. Strangely, the driver did not want me to help him carry the official into the apartment building. He said he could easily manage himself, but I noticed it was a struggle for him.

"Good-bye, my American friends," the official shouted so loudly that everyone on the street could hear him, "God bless America"; and he broke into a recognizable version of the *Star Spangled Banner*, substituting "da-da-da-da" for the words which he didn't know.

"I like him," I said to Leo. But there was no answer. Leo had, by this time, entered into the same condition as our Romanian friend.

The only difference was that Leo wasn't singing—he was snoring.

5. One, Two, Three...

In the preceding story of "The Tipsy Official," I mentioned the inspection trip to port cities on the Black Sea which I took with an official of a tire company. A year later, my company sold the same program to a company that manufactured television parts.

The trip participants were distributors from all over the U.S., and I made another inspection trip with an official of the sponsoring company.

In a meeting with one of the dockmaster's assistants in the port of Yalta in the Soviet

Union, we learned that the docks were busy the day our ship was scheduled to tie up.

I asked for the #1 berth, which would enable our guests to walk off the ship and be right in the center of Yalta. The other two docks were farther away, so I wanted to do everything I could to get the best space, especially as the group would not have a lot of time in this famous city.

The dockmaster's assistant, a jovial, round-faced fellow whose ruddy complexion betrayed his fondness for vodka, said he would do everything he could to give us the dock we wanted.

"By the way," he said, "would you mind bringing me some blue jeans and American rock records when you return with the group?"

"Sure," I said. "What size jeans?"

He replied that it didn't really matter, because he was going to sell them on the black market. "They're worth a great deal in the Soviet Union," he confessed.

I got the message. The chances of our getting the prime dock space on the date we wanted would be greatly enhanced if we were to give him the jeans and records. "This guy must have gotten his training in Chicago," I thought.

When the trip took place, I accompanied it as the trip director and flew in advance to Athens to check that everything was in readiness for the group's arrival two days later. In my luggage were three pairs of blue jeans and a half-dozen rock records.

As our ship approached Yalta, we were told to pull into berth #1, and, shortly afterwards, the dockmaster's assistant came aboard. I gave him the jeans and records as well as a couple of bottles of vodka.

"Oh, you are most kind," he spluttered, "most kind. How did you know I drank vodka?"

Then he told us that, while the ship was in the harbor, we were not allowed to flush the toilets. This, of course, presented quite a problem, but, surprisingly, the people took it well and treated it as a joke. We would be in port for only a few hours, and we urged our guests to make every effort to "hold it" until we went on the sightseeing tour and could use the rest rooms in town.

When our ship docked, we noticed about 150 people standing behind an iron barrier which had been erected to keep the Soviets from approaching the ship.

We were also informed that, as our visa was for a group visit, we should keep together and move as a group. The restriction that really bothered our group, however, was one that forbade us to "linger" at the barrier and thus prevent us from talking to the people.

The tour lasted about two hours, and everyone was returned to the ship to change for dinner. Before we disembarked, our Soviet guides led us to the restaurant, only a 10-

minute walk away.

By this time, the crowd at the barrier had grown considerably, no doubt drawn by a foreign ship and its American passengers, still a rarity in this part of the Soviet Union. They looked at us with sad faces but didn't make any move to communicate with us. At the end of the dock were two leather-coated men who followed us to the restaurant and back to the ship when we finished our meal.

On the return, however, many of the guests expressed a desire to talk to the people at the barrier. They were upset that this was not allowed and asked what would happen if they made contact.

"I don't think they can do much," I said. "We're leaving anyway, but they are aware that we can't speak Russian, and they are probably confident that their people can't speak English, so the officials feel fairly safe. But why not smile, wave to them and shake their hands?" I suggested.

And they did—with a big surprise. Some of the guests were Jewish, and they muttered a few words in Yiddish. Suddenly, the emotional dam burst, and a cacophonous din followed. There were about a dozen Jews among the Soviets, and animated conversation filled the air as our Jewish guests translated for the others.

One American woman took off her hat and presented it to a young woman, then kissed her on the cheek. Pens and cigarettes were given to the Soviets, and everyone wanted to touch each other.

It was simultaneously a happy and a tearful scene. Many of the Soviets cried, and some of our group unashamedly let the tears run down their cheeks, too.

Although the "leather coats" didn't make any attempt to stop the incident, they were moving around the people muttering to them, and I thought that, to spare the Russians some unpleasant moments afterwards, it would be better to board the ship.

As our liner slipped its moorings, the Russians sang a song to us. Our group was so taken aback that they just stood on the deck listening to them.

Then someone in our group started singing *God Bless America*, and everyone joined in until the Soviets were just a speck on the horizon.

But the trip was not without its humor. As the ship neared the harbor limits, the captain's voice came over the PA system:

"As we will leave the harbor of Yalta in just about five minutes, may I suggest you go to your cabins and, on my count of three, flush your toilets?"

Minutes later, the captain counted: "Ready now? One, two, three ... — and every toilet flushed into the Black Sea.

The Plaque

Visitors to my office usually comment on the striking plaque that hangs on my wall.

It has the bronzed front half of an elephant, its trunk raised in the symbol of good luck. A small brass plate, affixed to the plaque, reveals that I am an honorary member of the Mt. Kenya Safari Club, and is signed by Ray Ryan, the club president, and William Holden, its vice president.

The vice president whose signature appears on the plaque is that of the late

Hollywood actor. William Holden was a permanent resident of the Club and was one of its founders. He came to love Kenya so dearly that, in his later years, he left it for only three months each year to make one film.

I was the trip director for a group of elite automotive dealers and spouses who went on a photographic safari to Kenya in 1968. The chairman of the board and the president of the sponsoring company and their spouses accompanied the group, which numbered 34 people.

As a parenthetical item, I want to mention that when I say "elite" dealers, I mean elite! When the group arrived in Nairobi, the first item of business after they had taken a nap was to escort them to a tailor shop to be measured for safari outfits—khaki shirts, trousers, jungle boots and the inevitable pith helmets.

What's more, they didn't tramp through impenetrable jungle preceded by bearers with machetes hacking away at the growth. Oh, no, they were transported from one spot to another in air-conditioned Cadillacs. It got to be such a joke at the hotel that the front desk clerks, when they saw me approach, would say, "Here comes Bwana Pete, the fearless leader of that adventuresome safari group."

To return to the original story, a good trip director always looks for opportunities on site to improve a program without adding any cost.

I knew the manager of the Mt. Kenya Safari Club at that time, a wonderful gentleman by the name of Brian Burroughs, who had visited our offices in Detroit on a couple of occasions. I was aware that Holden lived on the property and so asked Brian if the actor was the amenable type who would be receptive to an invitation to attend the group's cocktail party that evening.

"He's a real down-to-earth guy," Brian told me. "Why don't you go down to his villa and ask him?"

Somewhat apprehensively, I walked to the villa, situated at the end of a row of beautiful cottages covered with the gorgeous flowers and plants indigenous to Africa.

My knock on the door was answered by Holden himself, clad in khaki shorts, a short-sleeved sports shirt and open-toed sandals. Very casual.

"Mr. Holden," I began, and went on to ask my request.

"Look, just call me Bill," he responded. "Sure, I'll be glad to attend for a few minutes anyway. Where is the cocktail party, at poolside?"

I nodded and gave him the time it would start.

The guests were totally unaware that so distinguished a personage would be joining us, and there was palpable excitement when he appeared.

Holden graciously took the time to have his photo taken with each couple. It amused me that several of the guests who had appeared so sophisticated and self-assured became flustered; some actually had goosebumps despite the warm temperature.

The actor invited me to join him and Brian for dinner that evening, which I had to turn down with great reluctance because my duties required my presence at the group banquet to ensure that everything went off without a hitch.

"Well, join us for a drink afterwards," he insisted, and I readily accepted.

It was an evening I will never forget. The chairman and president of the automobile company complimented me on having Holden attend the party. I was a hero.

When I met later with Bill and Brian in the latter's office, it was a laughfest from the second I arrived until the moment I left. They were great company, and I have many fond memories of our animated conversation, interspersed with jokes and funny incidents that had occurred at the Club.

Almost no mention was made of Holden's

movies; he preferred not to discuss his cellu-
loid life.

*   *   *

About six weeks later, back in Detroit, my
secretary brought in a large box that had
arrived in the mail from Kenya.

Inside was the plaque with the front of the
elephant and a note from Holden that simply
said:

Dear Pete,
    The next time you bring a group to
the Mt.Kenya Safari Club, I'll send you
the elephant's ass.

Sincerely,

Bill Holden

Sign Language

Every country in the world uses sign language—not the specific hand signals employed by the deaf and dumb, but those used by non-handicapped people who make formations by dexterously twisting the fingers in different ways to convey particular meanings.

For example, raising the thumb of your right hand indicates approval, while reversing the signal and pointing it to the ground means disapproval. Another is forming an "O" with the index finger and the thumb to mean "OK" or "good."

Most of these signs are universal. The "thumbs up" sign means the same in the U.S. as it does in Australia or Europe. There is, however, one country where sign language is totally different from that of any other, and that is Brazil. In fact, there are many more hand signals in Brazil than are used in any other country in the world.

If you are bothering a Brazilian, he is likely to rub the back of his fingers under his chin in a forward motion. This means "get lost." Or if you are talking to a Brazilian and not making any sense, he'll move his hand in a forward, circular motion meaning "you're talking a lot of nonsense."

*   *   *

Several years ago, we had a group in Rio and another member of our staff, Harry Miller, and I took the Convip and his wife to dinner when the group had a free evening. I asked our agent to make a reservation for us at one of the best restaurants in Rio.

It had been a delicious meal and everyone was in a convivial mood. When entertaining in such fashion, one is always anxious to make the evening a great success with a memorable meal, great atmosphere and enjoyable conversation.

It certainly had been a wonderful success and, at the end of the evening, I asked for the bill. The waiter brought it and asked if everything had been satisfactory. We assured him that the meal exceeded our expectations. His stiff and formal attitude indicated it was the only reply he ever received.

I noticed that he stopped to talk to the maître d' on his way to the cashier and, seconds later, the maître d' nodded over to Harry and me with a smile. Above the noise, his voice formed the words, "Was everything all right?"

Harry formed the universally (but not in Brazil) accepted "O" sign to express his approval.

The maître d's face froze, and he got visibly angry. He spoke to two other waiters and en masse they approached our table to vent their displeasure. One of the waiters who spoke excellent English said that their restaurant was not the type that attracted low-class people who made rude signs to the help, and that the maître d' would be pleased if we would pay our bill and leave immediately or we would be thrown out.

We stood there trying to figure out what had happened. We were explaining that we enjoyed the meal when the waiter intervened to suggest that, in the future, if we thought the food was delicious, to say so and not to exhibit immature behavior.

By this time, the Convip and his wife were becoming uncomfortable, and neither my colleague nor I could understand the sudden transformation from a glorious evening into one that was now approaching disaster.

The level of the waiters' and maître d's voices was now at a very high pitch and other diners were watching us with more than a little curiosity; many were anxious to know what had caused the altercation.

We paid the bill and took our leave as quickly as possible so as not to embarrass our guests any further.

The next morning, I repeated the incident to our land agent, who wanted to know exactly what we had done to incur the wrath of the restaurant's staff. He was concerned because it was he who had used his influence to obtain the reservation for us. It was a very high-class place, and he was understandably nervous that his reputation might have been compromised.

When Harry got to the point about using the "O" signal, the land agent moaned, "Oh, my God, do you know what that means? Have you any idea what you told the maître d' to do?"

Let me put it this way: In any other coun-

try in the world, as I have explained, the signal would have conveyed our complete satis-
faction with the meal and the service. In Rio,
however, the "O" signal is a suggestion to the
recipient that he go perform by himself a sex-
ual action that is physically impossible. Got
it? No? Then allow me to describe it euphem-
istically:

Our signal, as interpreted in Brazil, suggested to the maître d' that he go "stuff himself."

"*Jambo*"

One of the things I have noticed about Americans when they travel abroad is that they like to learn a few phrases in the language of the country they are visiting. In particular, they like to know "Thank you," "Please," "Hello" and "How are you." And then they memorize the phrases, learn how to pronounce them correctly and practice them whenever they can.

Conversely, I've noticed that natives enjoy it immensely when a visitor says a few words in their language. It opens up conversations and starts friendships.

We had a group in Kenya, one of my favorite countries. Its vast plains, incredibly blue skies and magnificent animals make it a destination that ranks among the most popular.

Whether you go on a tent or photographic safari, the beauty and mystique of Africa quickly become a part of you. I have seen skies at night all over the world, but I have never seen any with the clarity of those in Africa. The stars seem to have a special quality that makes them shine much brighter than anywhere else. The African skies have so many sidereal formations that it seems there are fewer dark spaces than bright ones.

In the story entitled "The Plaque," I wrote of an episode that involved William Holden, the actor, and mentioned the hilarious few hours I spent with him and Brian Burroughs, then the manager of the Mt. Kenya Safari Club.

In one of the few serious moments that night, Holden spoke almost religiously of his love of Africa and of the unshakeable hold it had on him. I don't think I fully understood what he meant until I had made another two or three trips to Kenya. Certainly I do now.

In our group, there was one tall, thin man, Ron Kraft, who found great pleasure in learning as many Swahili phrases as he could. (Swahili

is the language of Kenya, although English is spoken widely and is used in business.)

Wherever the group would go, Ron would ask questions in Swahili such as "How are you?" "Isn't it a lovely day?" The natives' faces would light up in obvious surprise and equal delight, and so Ron managed to make more friends in Nairobi than anyone else in the group.

The word for "Hello" in Swahili is "Jambo," an easy word to remember and even easier to pronounce. It is one of those all-encompassing words that also means "Good Day" and "How are you?"

The group had just returned to the Intercontinental Hotel in Nairobi from a "game run" in Nairobi National Park and were tired and ready for a nap before the evening's function.

We were waiting for an elevator when a black man in safari clothes stood beside us. Finally, the doors opened, people emerged and we entered.

Ron, nearest the control panel, asked everyone for their floors so that he could press the required buttons.

The black man didn't answer, so Ron turned to him and said, "Jambo." He was about to repeat his question when the man's face broke into a smile.

"What's with this Jambo shit, man?" he said. "I'm from Brooklyn."

Gentlemen Farmers

The Ritz Hotel in Lisbon was once ranked as the best hotel in the world. It is still considered among the top hostelries, although it lost its high ranking when it became a member of a well-known chain, and chain hotels are almost never accorded such a coveted title.

In the '60s when the incident I am about to describe occurred, the Ritz reigned supreme. It boasted elegant, high-ceilinged public rooms with objets d'art strewn around its hallways and rare tapestries adorning the walls of its lounges. All the richness, of course, is still there. It is not possible to find guest rooms that are better decorated or of a higher comfort level. The bathrooms are unbeatable in terms of opulence and style, with walls and floors of marble. If one was of a mind, a band could be hired to play in them and leave sufficient space to dance.

True to its undisputed claim of high quality, the bathrooms have separate areas for the bath, toilet and shower. I once had a client who hastily took a shower immediately after arriving from the States. He did not take the time to inspect the facilities properly, and assumed that a hand device attached to a perpendicular rod against the wall above the bath was the shower. The head slid up and down for a distance of 18 inches, with the maximum height about three feet above the tub. My client caustically commented to his wife that the shower must have been designed for midgets!

In January 1970, while based in London, I received a telex from my boss in the States asking me to perform a miracle. I was instructed to fly to Lisbon and use all my coercive powers to secure 75 rooms for a very important client. The incentive house for which I then worked planned to make a presentation to a seed company for a Lisbon-

Madeira program to take place in January 1971.

Performance of the miracle involved securing the rooms at the Ritz; the hotel did not accept groups. It was much too prestigious to have groups running around its quiet lobby and hallways. My company was told that, if we got the Ritz, we would get the business.

*   *   *

I flew to Lisbon and arranged an appointment with the general manager, a diminutive fellow who could easily have served as a model for royalty. He was a martinet, always immaculately attired in the typical hotel apparel of striped pants and black jacket with silver tie.

He was a man who seldom smiled, boasted a pencil-thin mustache and was very much the businessman. I had been introduced to him by our land agent in Portugal on a previous visit to the hotel and had met him again at a Tourist Office function in Lisbon, so we were slightly acquainted.

When I arrived at the Ritz, I had the concierge call the manager's office and apprise him of my arrival. A few minutes later, he met me in the lobby and suggested that we have coffee in the lounge.

We became seated at a window table over-

looking the gardens—an idyllic, peaceful setting and not at all compatible with the conversation that was to follow.

"What? Absolutely not," he said indignant-
ly, almost choking at the boldness of my
request. He shook his head vigorously, even
as I continued speaking and presenting what I
thought were cogent reasons why he should
accede to my plea.

"No, no, my dear sir," he said, "no, it is
quite out of the question. This is not one of
those convention hotels. This is the Ritz. We
do not take large groups. Maybe five or six
couples, but 75 rooms? No, I'm afraid not."

"But, Mr. Forleza," I continued, "they would
be coming in January, your quietest month."

"We are moderately busy in January," he
pointed out with some pride, anxious to
counter any valid argument. "This establish-
ment has its regular clientele who come here
from around the world for relaxation and
exquisite service. They don't want to push
through crowds to secure their room key, or to
take afternoon tea with raucous laughter and
loud voices interrupting the somnolence."

He was articulate and graphic in his
descriptions, but I was persistent. "Mr. Forleza
[I would never have dreamed of addressing
him by his first name, which, incidentally, I
did not know], these people are wealthy,

refined gentlemen. They are businessmen who are used to the very best. Our client has stayed many times in the Ritz (a mild assault on the truth!) and it was he who specifically asked for your hotel. He knows your high standards and is well aware of the decor and the reputation of the Ritz. He would never have asked for the Ritz if he thought his people would not fit in. The people he wants to bring are the 'creme de la creme'."

He did not respond immediately, and his silence encouraged me to press on, when suddenly a thought occurred to me.

"Mr. Forleza, what if we were to stagger the buses so that they were five minutes apart? This would mean that, on the transfers and tours, we would arrange it so that there would not be a sizable crowd at any one time in the lobby."

I had hit the mark. He was now listening attentively to what I was saying.

"That may work," he said with what for him amounted to enthusiasm. "Staggering the arrivals and departures of the buses, hmmmm?"

I had him reeling against the ropes; his defenses were down. Now for the coup de grace. "And we would use only the back door."

He stared aimlessly into space. There was silence for almost a minute. Then he nodded his head and said, "I think I will agree to your request with the suggestions you have made. Yes, I will allow it."

Bells and whistles sounded and fireworks exploded, if only in my mind. We went over all the stipulations once again as I excitedly wrote each one down.

I was ecstatic. I quickly called my office in Detroit and relayed the good news to them. They were incredulous. "You got the Ritz? Are you sure we're talking about the same hotel? The Ritz at the top of the Avenida da Liberdade?"

"Yes, yes, yes," I told them. I urged that the contract with all the agreements and the deposit be sent immediately. Normally we prepare a Letter of Agreement and send it to the client. When we receive the signed LOA and the client's check, we then forward the money to the hotel to confirm the group reservation.

This time, the procedures were reversed. We sent our check without waiting for the client's money. What had been accomplished was comparable to a journalist securing a national scoop.

*   *   *

Not every story has a happy ending, but this had a seriocomic one. After the trip oper-

Ritz
Dining Room
Hours: 7:00 AM to 10:00 PM

ated, I made a visit back to Detroit and, in the hallway, bumped into the trip director who had been in charge of the seed company's program.

"Oh, I have a message for you from Mr. Forleza," he said. "The next time he sees you, he plans to strangle you. He told me to tell you that there is a wide disparity between your comprehension of 'refined gentlemen' and his understanding of the words."

"What do you mean?" I inquired.

The trip director went on to explain that our "gentlemen" walked around the hotel with thick, plaid flannel shirts tucked inside blue jeans held up by multi-colored suspenders and wearing baseball caps touting the seed company's name.

Forleza also complained about their hobnailed boots destroying his carpets, their shouting in the lobby and lounges to attract one another's attention and making weird sounds more suited to "calling hogs than trying to communicate."

As it turned out, however, Mr. Forleza's main complaint was about the huge lines outside the breakfast restaurant at 6:30 A.M., waiting for the doors to open at 7:00 A.M., and the surging forward of the large crowd that bowled over the waiters when the doors were eventually unlocked.

Tarzan

We had a trip director named Bill Spencer who, in almost every respect, was good at his job. He had a glowing personality and an infectious charm that made people like him on first contact. He was pleasant, courteous and always willing to be helpful to the people in his groups.

But, like most people, Bill had an idiosyncrasy: he loved to imitate the jungle sounds of Tarzan, the Ape Man. This may not sound too disturbing except that he chose to do it when working on group trips and late at night when most people were sound asleep.

It was his habit to wake up the hotel with a loud, piercing yell whenever he returned late to his room. He would do it when the hotel was reasonably quiet and the guests had retired for the evening.

Most incentive trips are to resort facilities. Bill's *modus operandi* was to open his bedroom window and listen to the outside noises. When he could hear only the waves lapping the sandy beaches, the coquis chirping or the whistling toads calling their mates, he knew the propitious moment had arrived.

At that time, he would extinguish his room lights, approach the window and emit a strident call that, had he been in the jungle, would have drawn every elephant. Quickly, he would lower his window and stand back in the darkness to observe the reaction.

Lights would be turned on, windows would be raised and heads would pop out to see if the Ape Man could be located. I recall one occasion when, sharing a room with Bill, I saw him wait for someone to emerge from a window. He then opened ours and, seeing the other person, shouted out, "I don't think that's very funny at this time in the morning."

The innocent person would sputter in embarrassment: "It wasn't I; I didn't do it. I was trying to find the one who woke *me* up."

The Tarzan Yell was always a topic of discussion at the breakfast table next morning.

"Did you hear that idiot yelling last night?" one would ask.

"We should complain to the management," was another oft-made statement.

"It was probably some drunk with that convention group," another would offer as an explanation.

Bill would be sure to join some of the trip participants at breakfast and raise the subject of the "Yell," if someone didn't beat him to it. If one of our esteemed competitors also had a group in the hotel, Bill would proffer the suggestion that their trip directors were a wild bunch, and he wouldn't be surprised if it was they who were doing it.

Surprisingly, Bill was never caught, although he knew there were many people waiting behind windows in the darkness for the errant jungle warrior to make a slip. I'm quite sure that, if he had ever been found out, he would have been expelled from the hotel and subsequently fired. But he loved the challenge and he thrived on danger. Of course, all of our trip directors knew he was the Tarzan imitator but kept his secret.

When the third or fourth night of a trip had been reached, Bill would leave the window raised before going to dinner, thus eliminating the need to fuss with it (and alert the vigilant guests) when he returned.

Once back in his room, he would not turn on the lights. Slinking over to the window and making sure he could not be seen, he would listen for the sounds of silence.

Then he would make the roar that has been imitated by every schoolboy since Edgar Rice Burroughs' Ape Man first reached the movie screens. Heads would be thrust out of windows to commiserate with one another, knowing full well that Tarzan had once again escaped their detection.

Bill often joined the frustrated guests in their animated window conversations. He even shouted out, "Okay, smart-aleck [he had to watch his language in front of the guests, although theirs was certainly not free of epi-thets!] we've had enough. Some of us aren't here on vacation and have to work. We need our sleep. Knock it off because, if I find you, you won't be able to make *any* kind of sound."

The other guests would cheer and applaud Bill. The next morning, he was always a hero.

There was one occasion when his antic turned into something even more funny. It occurred in the British Colonial Hotel in Nassau, a downtown property situated on a beautiful white, sandy beach. Bill had left his win-

dow open on this particular evening, which was the final night of the trip.

I was rooming with him once again and, when we entered the room, he said, "Don't put on the lights. I want to give Tarzan a chance to say good-bye to his subjects."

*   *   *

We undressed in the dark and brushed our teeth. As I jumped into my bed, Bill let go with a yell that must have stirred all the animals in far-off Africa.

About ten seconds elapsed before the silence was broken by a voice from the garden area below. The slurred speech suggested the respondent was in a tipsy condition as he shouted up to the heavens:

"Jump, Tarzan! I'll catch you!"

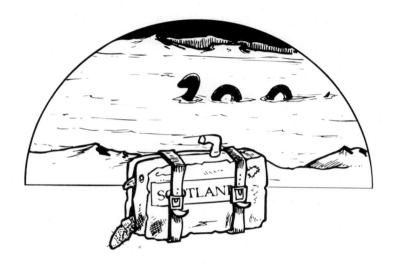

The Gowffing Trip

Incentive programs are almost never designed around a specific sport for the simple reason that it is highly unlikely that the broad spectrum of people to whom the program is being offered would all like that sport. An incentive program must offer something that appeals to everyone.

When London or Hong Kong is the destination, the sponsoring company can safely assume that close to 95 per cent of all eligible participants love to travel. But if it's a skiing

trip to Colorado, it's a safe bet that only 20
per cent would put forth that extra effort and
work the long hours required to achieve the
prize.

In other words, everybody loves to travel,
but not everybody loves to ski, or fish or play
tennis.

On only one occasion can I ever remember
an incentive program being sponsored with a
sport as the theme, and that was a golfing trip
to Scotland in 1968.

The president of the incentive company for
which I worked at the time called me into his
office and suggested (a euphemism for
ordered) that I assign myself as the trip director on a tour to Scotland which was being
sponsored by an automobile company. The
trip was a specially-designed one, and the
chairman of the board and president of the
automobile company planned to join the 15
winning couples.

So unique was the program that the campaign rules specifically mentioned that only the
first 15 dealers—not 17 or 16—but *15* would
qualify and be accompanied by their spouses.

A special feature of the program was the
inclusion of Mike Souchak, one of the best golf
professionals in the '60s, who was to accompany the group and play each day with the
dealers.

In his heyday, Mike was not only a very popular golfer, but it was said he could easily have become one of the most successful were it not for the fact that he did not have the big-match temperament. He had forearms like tree trunks and could slam a ball farther than any of his peers.

He had all the other golfing skills too, but when he played in the national tournaments, the pressure adversely affected his abilities. As a result, he didn't capture as many of the big prizes as his talents deserved.

The program called for the group to stay three nights at the magnificent Gleneagles Hotel near the city of Perth, Scotland. Gleneagles, at that time, had three championship courses. Now it has four. It is a golfer's paradise that draws ardent practitioners of the sport from around the world.

The next stop for the group was the equally beautiful Turnberry Hotel, where three more nights would allow the dealers to play on its two championship courses.

Mike mentioned that this was his first trip to Scotland and, because it is the home of golf (or gowff, as it is known in the Scottish dialect), was the fulfillment of a dream for him. As a matter of interest, Mike also disclosed after the trip that Turnberry was the finest course he had ever played!

While staying at Gleneagles and at Turnberry, Mike was besieged by other guests for
his autograph. Kids in the street easily recognized him and would proffer a piece of paper
and plead for his signature. No matter where
Mike would go, everyone knew who he was
and wanted to talk to him.

Of course, it should be pointed out that,
while the dealers were playing golf, special
shopping and sightseeing tours were arranged
for non-players, who were accorded royal treat-
ment and transported in luxurious limousines.

On the last morning of our stay at Gleneagles, as we prepared to transfer to Turnberry, it had been arranged for the group to
stop in St. Andrews and play a round on the
hallowed turf of the Old Course which is adjacent to the Royal and Ancient Club—a must
for any golfer.

It may come as a surprise to all but the
most fervent golfers to learn that the Old
Course, the first ever built, is public. It is not
owned by a country club or special organiza-
tion. Anyone may play on it, and the greens
fees have always been relatively low when
compared with other famous courses in the
world. In 1968, at the time of this incident,
the greens fees were only 75 cents! Today they
are about $70, still much less than most
courses.

The Old Course has a special appeal because every golfing great who ever lived has played its 18 holes, and it is a goal of every true golfer to drive off its first tee.

En route from Gleneagles to the beautiful little town of St. Andrews, I rode in one of the limousines with Mike.The program called for the group to have a tour of the Royal and Ancient Club's museum, which houses the original rules of golf, some of the first clubs ever used and a plethora of memorabilia of the game which is now played in just about every country in the world.

"Say, when the others are going through the R and A, why don't we have a cup of coffee?" Mike suggested.

I was taken aback. "Why?" I asked. "Don't you want to see the historical items and rare photographs of the sport?"

"Of course I do," he replied, "but they won't let professionals in the Club. It's an old R and A rule."

I was not aware of such a restriction, and I confessed so to Mike. Nevertheless, he assured me, such a rule did indeed exist. (Incidentally, at one time the Club also forbade ladies to play on the course. Fortunately, both rules have been relaxed. Professionals may now tour the museum, and ladies can frequently be seen on the course, ofttimes posting better scores than the men!)

"Well, why don't you just join the group and, if they do stop you, then we can go and have coffee," I suggested.

Mike laughed gently. "What chance do you think I would have?" he asked. "We're in the home of golf and, everywhere we've been, you've noticed how I've been surrounded by adults and kids. This is the home of golf, and they really take it seriously here."

Of course, he was right.

"Well, why not take a chance anyway," I countered. "You said you would love to see the museum, so it's worth a try."

I convinced him to do it, and he moved right through the museum without any of the ticket takers and ushers recognizing him.When the group finished the tour, I approached Mike to ask if anyone had said anything to him.

"Would you believe it?" he asked, a smile creasing his face. "Everywhere in Scotland I've been recognized—shops, hotels, restaurants, on tours. The only place I *wasn't* known was in the golf museum of the Royal and Ancient Club in St. Andrews, the very place where golf began!"

He slowly shook his head, the dealers roared and everyone moved to the first tee.

Additional copies of *Humor Travels Well* are available from:

Galde Press, Inc.
PO Box 65611
St. Paul, MN 55165

Please send $5.95 for each copy, plus $1.50 shipping and handling. Minnesota residents include 6.5 % sales tax.